THE WAY OF THE
MARKSMEN

Copyright © 2025 by Richard Hernandez

Published by Arrows & Stones

All rights reserved. No portion of this book may be reproduced, stored in a retrieval system, or transmitted in any form or by any means—electronic, mechanical, photocopy, recording, scanning, or other—except for brief quotations in critical reviews or articles, without prior written permission of the author.

Scripture quotations marked NIV are taken from the Holy Bible, New International Version®, NIV®. Copyright © 1973, 1978, 1984, 2011 by Biblica, Inc.™ Used by permission of Zondervan. All rights reserved worldwide. www.zondervan.com. The "NIV" and "New International Version" are trademarks registered in the United States Patent and Trademark Office by Biblica, Inc.™ | Scripture quotations marked NKJV are taken from the New King James Version®. Copyright © 1982 by Thomas Nelson. Used by permission. All rights reserved. | Scripture quotations marked MSG are taken from THE MESSAGE, copyright © 1993, 1994, 1995, 1996, 2000, 2001, 2002 by Eugene H. Peterson. Used by permission of NavPress. All rights reserved. Represented by Tyndale House Publishers, Inc.

For foreign and subsidiary rights, contact the author.

Cover design by Sara Young

ISBN: 978-1-964794-45-7   1 2 3 4 5 6 7 8 9 10

Printed in the United States of America

WHAT PEOPLE ARE SAYING ABOUT
THE WAY OF THE MARKSMEN

Pastor Richard Hernandez has combined his entrepreneurial skills with his pastoral heart in *The Way of the Marksmen*. His step-by-step approach to discipleship is based on both personal experience and biblical principles. Pastor Hernandez's vulnerability pulls the reader in to hit the bullseye in their walk with Jesus. As you read *The Way of the Marksmen*, take heart, take aim, and prepare yourself for a targeted read on loving Jesus.

—Rev. Bret Allen
District Superintendent
Northern California and Nevada Assemblies of God

Picture a UFC fight. The announcer enters the middle of the ring. The crowd is on its feet, the microphone turned to its maximum volume, and he screams, "It's time!" What time is it? Time for real men to display what it means to be a man of God to a confused generation: sharing Jesus with their coworkers, in the church, and at the altar during worship with hands raised. Supporting the ministry of the church. Dressing for battle with the anointing to conquer. Who cares what society thinks? A lion does not lose sleep over the opinions of sheep. Pastor Richard Hernandez has written a "right now, today" word for men to become marksmen. God has given men a target to take our families back, our cities back, and our nation back. Life has no remote control; you have to get up and change it yourself.

—Glen Berteau
Father of the House Modesto Churches
Servant, Author, Pastor, Evangelist

I have known Richard Hernandez for over twenty-five years. He is a man who lives out his beliefs, and in his new book, *The Way of the Marksmen*, he shares personal stories and practical insights from his experiences as a husband, father, businessman, and pastor. Richard doesn't shy away from sharing his struggles, openly discussing his challenging upbringing and his battles with depression and burnout. As he says in the book, "I'm writing this book to help other men avoid paying for knowledge with blood, sweat, and tears." Richard's unique perspective of ministry and the business world shines through in his writing. He understands the pressures men face today and offers practical guidance on navigating those challenges while remaining true to their faith. This is not a simple "self-help" book; in his own words, it is a book that will "help you discover the kind of man God wants you to be." That's his pastor's heart showing.

Richard uses the analogy of a marksman aiming at a target. Just like a marksman needs focus and discipline to hit the bullseye, we, too, need clear direction and practical steps to reach our goals in life, and Richard's book provides just that. You won't find empty words or feel-good slogans here; instead, he offers a clear path for men who want to grow in their faith, lead their families, and make a difference in the world. I highly recommend *The Way of the Marksmen* to men who long to deepen their faith, strengthen their families, and make a real difference in the world.

—Pastor Larry Neville
President PC Global Network
Praise Chapel International
www.pcglobalnetwork.com

THE WAY OF THE MARKSMEN

A MEN'S GUIDE TO FOLLOWING JESUS

RICHARD HERNANDEZ

I dedicate this book to my wife, Katrina, who has been with me every step of this journey—enduring the difficult early years and sharing in every success and failure. I couldn't do this without you. I also dedicate this to my late Pastor Mitch Thurman, who believed in me when others saw only a street kid and high school dropout. Thank you for seeing my potential and investing in me; your legacy lives on through this book.

CONTENTS

Acknowledgments xi
Introduction 13

PART 1. THE WAY OF A MARKSMAN 17

CHAPTER 1.   **NORTH Put God First** 19
CHAPTER 2.   **SOUTH Deny Self** 33
CHAPTER 3.   **EAST   Part A: Value Family** 47
CHAPTER 4.   **WEST   Part B: Uphold Ministry** 59

PART 2. THE MEASURE OF A MARKSMAN 67

CHAPTER 5.   **The Fear of God** 71
CHAPTER 6.   **Know the Word** 83
CHAPTER 7.   **Mature as Men** 99
CHAPTER 8.   **Know Who You Are** 115
CHAPTER 9.   **Be Like Jesus** 127

PART 3. THE CHARACTER OF A MARKSMAN 141

CHAPTER 10. **Men of Integrity** 143
CHAPTER 11. **Men of Humility** 151
CHAPTER 12. **Men of Courage** 157
CHAPTER 13. **Men of Compassion** 169
CHAPTER 14. **Men of Faith** 181
CHAPTER 15. **It All Comes Together** 191

ACKNOWLEDGMENTS

I would like to acknowledge my family—my sons Nicholas, Isaiah, and Samuel, my daughter Leticia, and my grandchild Ezekiel. You enrich my life and motivate me to grow and become a better person and provider.

I'm grateful for the leaders who have poured into me over the years: Pastor Larry Neville, Dr. Samuel Huddleston, and our District Superintendent, Brett Allen—your examples of leadership have deeply shaped me, and I'm thankful for each of you.

To my friends who have stood by me, including our dedicated church staff, Diana, Steven, and Chris—your efforts have made all of this possible.

To my friend Adriel Cruz, your ministry and creativity inspire me.

Pastor Derik from Rise City Church, your friendship and partnership have helped pave the way for this book.

Pastor Jim Uhey, thank you for always believing in me.

Tony Sandoval, thank you for coming alongside me in the right season.

To Pastors Albert and Lynette, Al and Gloria Perez, Pastor Nora Soulik, Guillermo, and Tomas—thank you for standing strong with me in this new launch.

Special thanks to Pastor Dale Reece, who has been more than a mentor and friend. Without you, I'm not sure we would have made it this far.

Myra and Kathy Green, thank you for your support.

To my congregation at Family Life—you are the reason we do this. I'm so thankful for all of you.

INTRODUCTION

I've been pastoring for many years, and one of the most challenging yet crucial tasks is to raise up and disciple strong men in the church. Over time, I have witnessed a trend; women tend to serve, bond, and get involved more naturally, while men hesitate and need a push. However, when you can genuinely engage men, something extraordinary happens. The community is completely transformed for the better.

I have found that men need direction—clear, concise goals to aim for. We want to be part of something meaningful and connected, but we don't always know how. We often struggle to be ourselves, open up, and trust. It's one thing to trust God; it's another to trust other men, especially when we've been let down or hurt in the past.

I know this struggle personally. My relationship with my father wasn't great—not because he didn't want it to be but because he was battling his own demons, including drug addiction and unresolved trauma that caused him to be violent, abusive, and emotionally absent. When I encountered Christ, I knew that the cycle needed to be broken. Even with faith, it took me years to unpack the layers of pain and baggage I had collected. We often don't realize how our relationship with our earthly father can affect how we relate to our heavenly Father.

I believe the concepts in this book will help you discover the kind of man God wants you to be. Men must understand that it's not enough to identify as Christians—we are called to be disciples and leaders. We cannot carry on Jesus's work with weak men, hurt men who hurt others, or men who have no direction. You can't lead when you are lost. We need men who know where they're going and are willing to do the hard work to get there.

This book will give you a basic plan to direct your path—a path we call *The Way of the Marksmen*. For many reasons, I was inspired while watching the 2024 Olympics, which turned out to be a historic event. As a Warriors fan, I'll never forget Steph Curry's legendary shooting performance, even though I was forced to watch it on my phone. I was at an outdoor clay pigeon range with a group of men for an outing that was scheduled before we knew the game would be on. The Olympic shooting event frequently referenced how hard the sport was, and those seeds were being planted as I held my shotgun, trying to hit my targets. What surprised me was how the shooting competition went viral—there was something about it that resonated with me. I did not even know it was an Olympic sport, and at the time, we needed to ignite a spark within the men of our church. All these little signs got me thinking about how difficult it is to consistently hit the mark—both in shooting and in life—and that's when the Marksmen Men's Ministry, built on the concept of direction and purpose built on faith and accountability, was birthed. The concept explores knowing the direction and hitting our target. Being on the Olympic stage takes a lot of effort and clear direction on what you need to become the very best at what you do. Every Olympic athlete works hard and has a clear direction to earn their place on stage.

The name "Marksmen" represents a group of Christian men focused on living with purpose and precision, much like a marksman aiming at a target. We are called to fix our eyes on Jesus (Hebrews 12:2) and to press on toward the goal of godliness (Philippians 3:14). Achieving this requires discipline, training, and accountability, sharpening one another in faith.

This book will explore what it means to become Marksmen of Faith. The book is set up in three parts: *The Way of a Marksman, The Measure of a Marksman,* and *The Character of a Marksman.*

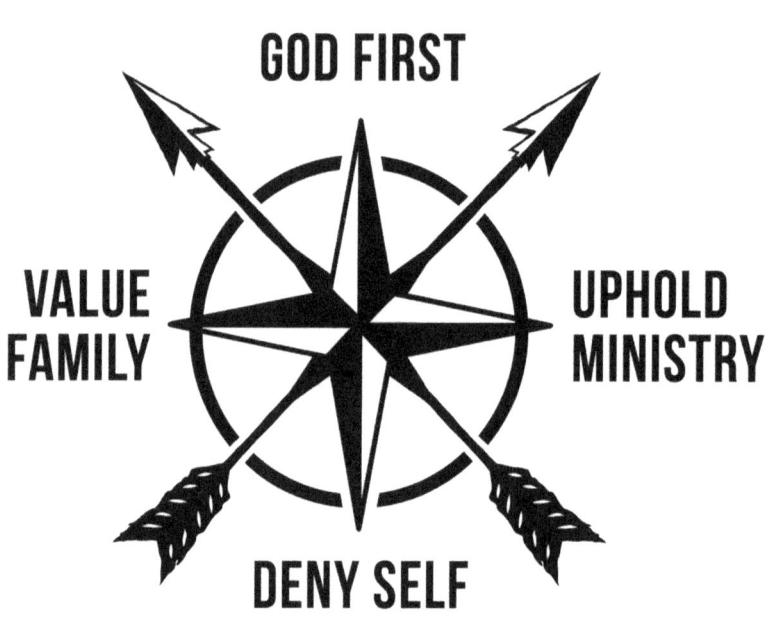

PART 1
THE WAY OF A MARKSMAN

Men need and should have direction before they can start building anything. Many of us, especially when we are young, like to get started before we know what we are doing and figure it out along the way.

I remember when I was a young man, I would talk about all the things I wanted to accomplish and the things I wanted to buy, but I wasn't doing anything to achieve those dreams. I ended up a high school dropout with no education and no direction. But then I went to church, received the Lord, and everything changed. I thank God that it happened so early in my life—right after getting kicked out of high school. I got saved the same year at sixteen. I quickly learned that faith could work wonders and that I could accomplish anything if I was willing to put Him first in my life. Even with that understanding, I faced the challenge of staying on the right path and consistently moving in the right direction for years.

When you need to know where you're going, you need a reference point—a tool to guide you. Whether you use a landmark, a map, or directions from someone else, you need direction. A compass is crucial for telling you whether you are heading in the right direction. I remember getting my driver's license before GPS was in every car and on every phone. Often, I would find myself driving the wrong way down the highway because I lacked a sense of direction. The Bible points to Jesus, and Jesus shows us the way because He is the way, the truth, and the life (John 14:6). As men, the key is to learn what it means to follow Jesus.

The Way of the Marksmen is about knowing whom you're following and keeping the right balance for your life to move forward. The four compass points—north, south, east, and west—help us navigate in the right direction. Similarly, the four principles I'll share in this section will guide you in life.

There's an old stereotype that men hate asking for directions, but it is better to know where you're going and be prepared and equipped than to figure it out along the way and make wrong turns. Here is the reality. If you don't know, then ask, seek, get direction—do whatever it takes! The Bible says, "If any of you lacks wisdom, let him ask God" (James 1:5, ESV).

The Way of the Marksmen establishes the foundational principles of guiding your walk with God. It answers the "how" of the journey—how to center your life around these four main principles: putting God first, denying self, valuing family, and upholding the ministry. Just like a compass pointing true north, these principles need to stay in balance for you to keep heading in the right direction. Now that we've laid the groundwork, the following chapters will explore these four foundational principles in greater depth. You'll see how each one serves as a directional guide in your life, helping you aim for the bullseye—becoming more like Jesus.

CHAPTER 1
NORTH PUT GOD FIRST

Putting God first is often easier said than done. Men have various interpretations of what it means to truly prioritize God in our lives. Many of us may say that God is first, but our actions and priorities don't always reflect that statement. It's important to remember that actions will always speak louder than words. The church today doesn't need more Christian commentators—we need more Christian examples. One reason men struggle with putting God first is that we often value the wrong things: gifts over fruit, physical strength over spiritual strength, and confidence or cockiness over humility. This backward thinking can interfere with our ability to surrender to God fully. The reality is that many of us have idols in our lives—things we value more than God. These idols become obstacles to making God first in our hearts.

DEFINING IDOLATRY

The Bible warns us about idols because they can take God's rightful place in our hearts. But idolatry isn't just about worshiping statues or false gods like we see in the Bible. An idol can be anything we prioritize or value more than God. It can be our job, a relationship, money, entertainment, or even ourselves. When something other than God occupies the top spot in our lives, it becomes an idol.

The prophet Ezekiel said, "Son of man, these leaders have set up idols in their hearts. They have embraced things that will make them fall into sin" (Ezekiel 14:3).

Idolatry isn't just a physical act of bowing down to something. It's a heart issue—placing something or someone above God. When that happens, we no longer trust Him fully, and our relationship with Him suffers, ultimately leading us back into sin.

THE DANGERS OF IDOLATRY

To illustrate, let me give you a personal example. I'm a massive football fan, specifically, a Raiders fan. For years, my mood lived and died with the outcome of their games. If they lost, my whole day would be ruined. If they won, I'd celebrate—but not always in a healthy way. You'd think this would change when I became a Christian, but at first, it didn't. For years, I didn't even realize that football had become an idol in my life. Initially, I only missed church on Sundays to watch big games. When I finally felt convicted, I recorded and watched the games later. But before the service ended, someone would always tell me the score, and I'd get angry again. The issue wasn't just about football; it went deeper. I had a lot of unresolved anger, and football became my outlet, an idol I ran to when I needed an excuse to indulge my impulses or release unwanted emotions. I could get into the game and, for a brief moment, forget everything else going on.

The anger I felt wasn't directed at the Raiders for losing but at everyone else who crossed my path that day. The pattern of lashing out in anger wasn't isolated to football; it also showed up in my relationships and other areas of my life. We often think these hobbies or vices are harmless because, on the surface, there's nothing wrong with enjoying football. I still love football—my cars are silver and black, and my nephew even played for the Raiders in the NFL. I'm closer to the game than ever because of his ten-year career in the league. I enjoy football. However, I had a season when I needed to first address how it had become an idol. I stopped watching; I missed just about every game, and I was still okay. Once I realigned my life and put God first, I was able to enjoy football in a healthy way, and more importantly, it no longer usurped God as my top priority.

Following Jesus can sometimes mean giving things up—whether temporarily or permanently. It can be hard to hear when He asks us to let go, but all I can say is to trust Him. The outcome will always be for your best.

The Rich Young Ruler (Mark 10:17-27)

A biblical example of this struggle is found in the story of the rich young ruler in Mark 10. This man wanted to follow Jesus, but one thing stood in the way—his wealth. When Jesus told him to sell everything he had and follow Him, the man walked away sad because he couldn't let go of his possessions:

> *Looking at the man, Jesus felt genuine love for him. "There is still one thing you haven't done," he told him. "Go and sell all your possessions and give the money to the poor, and you will have treasure in heaven. Then come, follow me." At this, the man's face fell, and he went away sad, for he had many possessions.* —Mark 10:21-22

Like this man, we often elevate things in our lives—whether wealth, hobbies, or relationships—above God. Jesus calls us to let go of these idols so we can follow Him fully.

> **Jesus wasn't trying to strip him of joy; Jesus was trying to open his eyes to something greater.**

Now, depending on how you read this story—whether you're an optimist or a pessimist—you might wonder: *why did Jesus ask him to sell everything?* Did he want him to be poor, stay poor, or something else? Could it be that the true riches Jesus tried to give him had nothing to do with money? I believe that Jesus knew wealth wasn't fulfilling this man, and by letting it go—whether temporarily or permanently—he would find a far more fulfilling life than by holding onto his possessions. Jesus wasn't trying to strip him of joy; Jesus was trying to open his eyes to something greater. This is what God calls us to when He says, "Follow me."

Reflection Question: What might you be holding onto that is preventing you from fully following Jesus? How can you begin to let go of it today?

GIDEON

I also think of the story of Gideon. In Judges 6, we find Gideon hiding in a winepress, threshing wheat secretly because he was afraid of the Midianites, who were oppressing Israel. Gideon was from the weakest tribe in Israel and even described himself as the least in his family. When the angel of the Lord appeared to him, the way the angel greeted him seemed like a mistake, as he called him "a mighty man of valor" (Judges 6:12, ESV).

How could this be? Gideon certainly didn't look like a mighty man. He was hiding in fear, full of doubt about whether God was really with his people. But God didn't see Gideon as the man hiding and afraid at that moment—He saw who Gideon could become if he followed Him. God saw beyond his fear and insecurity to the man of courage and faith that He would raise up to deliver Israel. Despite his doubts and questions, Gideon listened to the Lord. In Judges 6:14-16, the Lord tells Gideon:

> *"Go with the strength you have, and rescue Israel from the Midianites. I am sending you!"*
>
> *"But LORD," Gideon replied, "how can I rescue Israel? My clan is the weakest in the whole tribe of Manasseh, and I am the least in my entire family!"*
>
> *The LORD said to him, "I will be with you. And you will destroy the Midianites as if you were fighting against one man."*

This conversation with God shows us a powerful truth: when God calls us, He equips us. Gideon didn't need to be strong on his own; he simply needed to trust in the strength and guidance of God. Despite his fear and uncertainty, Gideon chose to follow God's command.

Here is an essential truth connected to this story: the first thing God asked Gideon to do wasn't to fight a battle—it was to tear down the idols in his own community. He had to start with his own house before Gideon could lead his people to victory. In Judges 6:25-26, God says:

> *"Take the second bull from your father's herd, the one that is seven years old. Pull down your father's altar to Baal, and cut down the Asherah pole standing beside it. Then, build an altar to the LORD your God here on this hilltop sanctuary, laying the stones carefully. Sacrifice the bull as a burnt offering on the altar, using as fuel the wood of the Asherah pole you cut down."*

This was a challenging task. Gideon was afraid of what his family and the people in his town would do if they found out, so he did it at night. But he still obeyed God, and that act of obedience was the first step toward becoming the mighty man of valor God had called him to be.

Like Gideon, we can't put God first and hold onto our idols. Before Gideon could lead his people into battle and victory, he had to address the idols in his own life and community. And that's where many of us find ourselves. We want God's blessing; we want to walk in victory, but we're still holding onto things that take the place of God in our hearts. Jesus reminds us of this same truth in Matthew 10:37, where He says, "If you love your father or mother more than you love me, you are not worthy of being mine, or if you love your son or daughter more than me, you are not worthy of being mine."

Jesus isn't saying that we shouldn't love our families. He's showing us that God must come first. When we allow anything—whether it's family, career, money, or hobbies—to become more important than God, we miss the fullness of what He wants to do in our lives.

When we look at Gideon, we see a powerful example of what happens when we follow God's direction, tear down the idols, and trust Him fully. Gideon went from hiding in fear to leading three hundred men to defeat an enemy because God was with him. He may not have felt like a mighty man of valor when he was hiding in that winepress. Still, God saw his potential, and through obedience, Gideon stepped into becoming the man he was called to be. Walking the path God has for us will require faith, and most importantly, you need direction on where you are going—a clear path by removing idols that are in your way.

Reflection Questions:
- What is the one thing you might be placing above God in your life? It could be something as big as your career or as small as your daily habits.
- How has this "idol" impacted your relationship with God and others? What changes do you need to make to shift your focus?

PRACTICAL APPLICATION
STEPS TO IDENTIFYING IDOLS

1) **Evaluate Your Time and Priorities:** Where do you spend most of your time? What's the first thing you think about when you wake up and the last thing you think about before you sleep? These questions may point to idols.
2) **Consider Your Emotions:** How would you react if something you care about were taken away? Our emotional response to losing something can reveal its true importance.
3) **Pray for Clarity:** Ask God to reveal anything in your heart that has taken His place. Pray as David did in Psalm 139:23-24: "Search me, O God, and know my heart; test me and know my anxious thoughts. Point out anything in me that offends you and lead me along the path of everlasting life."

MAKING GOD LORD OF YOUR LIFE

Putting God first means making Him not just your Savior but also your Lord. It means He's more than just a helper or healer—He becomes the very direction and inspiration for your life. We don't get to pick and choose the parts of His Word that suit our wants and dreams. Instead, we must look to His teachings to guide every area of our lives.

Jesus said in Matthew 6:33: "Seek the Kingdom of God above all else, and live righteously, and he will give you everything you need."

Putting God first means trusting that when we prioritize Him, everything else will fall into place—our relationships, our careers, and our purpose. When God is first in our lives, everything else becomes secondary, and our lives find their actual direction.

MY STORY: PUTTING GOD FIRST

I've seen the rewards of putting God first in my own life. I mentioned that I was a high school dropout with no direction. But everything changed when I started to put God at the center of my decisions. I became a business owner and a homeowner in Silicon Valley. I built a multimillion-dollar company and was blessed with a wonderful wife and four great kids. But here's the truth: none of those achievements mean anything compared to the most significant thing I've ever become—a faithful follower of Jesus.

The fulfillment I've found in following Christ far surpasses any worldly success. When God is first, everything else falls into place. I don't say this to boast but to show you what's possible when you make Him the foundation of your life. God took a man with no education, prospects, or direction and turned him into someone who leads in business, family, and ministry—all because I learned to put Him first.

> Blood, sweat, and tears may be the currency by which wisdom is purchased.

Now, that might sound simple—maybe even too simple. But the truth is, it's not easy at all. There's a constant struggle with pride, personal issues, and self-doubt. Neither my hardships nor my successes appeared out of nowhere— they built up over time.

It took a long time to get things right, and I am still working through many areas to this day. I might've taken a shorter path if I'd spent more time listening and studying earlier. But some of us, myself included, must learn the hard way. That's the only school I've known—the school of hard knocks.

I've written this book to help other men avoid paying for knowledge with blood, sweat, and tears. However, that might not always be avoidable because, in reality, wisdom often comes at a cost. In fact, blood, sweat, and tears may be the currency with which wisdom is purchased. Following Jesus has a price. Putting God first comes with a price.

My breakthrough didn't happen overnight. Yes, the Holy Spirit was at work in my life, but I had to do some real hard work, including seeking counseling. Some things changed quickly, while others were buried deep inside for years. I hope you take no offense from this, but it's a reality I lived with—and maybe many of you deal with the same. I'm going to speak plainly. As the son of a Hispanic gang member growing up around other Hispanics, we didn't talk about seeking help or counseling. In my family, emotions were seen as a sign of weakness, so every feeling I had came out as anger. I didn't know how to process complex emotions. Truthfully, I acted like a child—throwing emotional tantrums, often outbursts of rage, all filtered through this deep-rooted anger, even towards the people I loved. Childish emotions appear when we walk down the wrong path for so long that our priorities and responses get out of order. We don't know how to make the right decisions, especially in times of high stress. As men, we can't live that way.

It wasn't until I started looking at Jesus's example in Scripture that I was able to humble myself and let Him change my heart. One of the most freeing passages for men in the entire Bible is also the shortest: "Jesus wept" (John 11:35). Think about that. Not only did Jesus weep, but He did it in front of other men. Hopefully, a light bulb just went off in your mind—it's okay to let your guard down and express how you feel.

It's because we are weak that Jesus needed to come in the first place. Romans 5:6 says, "When we were utterly helpless, Christ came at just the right time and died for us sinners." Our weakness and inability to save ourselves is why we need Jesus. The Bible further reminds us in 2 Corinthians 12:9, "My power works best in weakness." God's power is most evident when we recognize our limitations and depend on Him. This passage doesn't excuse us to be weak men—it's the opposite. It reminds us that our strength doesn't come from ourselves but from God. When we face our own limitations, it's an opportunity to lean into God's grace and power, allowing Him to work through us. As we rely on His strength, we can overcome what we could never handle on our own.

It would be impossible for me to be a good husband, a good father, a successful businessman, and a leader in ministry in my own strength. Even though I have the Holy Spirit, I still have a sinful nature. I'm still human—I have a limited mind and emotions. But the good news is, I don't rely on my own strength. I have access to God, not because of anything I've done, but because Jesus made a way for me.

That's my motivation. That's why I know I can put God first. Even when I stray off the path, I know I can get back on track because it's never been about my strength in the first place.

God gives us a choice—follow Him or stay the same. The power of choice defines us as men. God won't choose for us because then it wouldn't be real. The ability to choose is a gift that proves we are indeed men created in His image.

Our emotions don't lead us to righteousness. As James 1:20 says, "Human anger does not produce the righteousness God desires." This passage tells me I can't rely on myself to get it right. I need to tap into something beyond me—the power of God.

That's why I'm encouraged. I'm not fighting against my bad habits on my own. I have an Advocate, a Champion in my corner—and so do you. It may feel like you have a long way to go, and maybe you do, but true marksmen, strong in faith, will do everything they can to get back on the right path.

As you read this book, I pray that you will adopt the same mindset—that God created you as a man for a higher purpose. There will be times in your life when you will question that. You will wonder, *Did God really call me? Did He really say that about me? Am I on the right path?* That's when you need your compass. That's when you search your heart and look for "True North," asking, *Is God first in my life?*

Reflection Questions:

- What would your life look like if you truly put God first in every area?
- In what specific areas of your life are you tempted to take control instead of letting God lead?

TAKE OWNERSHIP

Putting God first isn't just a one-time decision—it's a daily commitment. It means making Jesus the Lord of your entire life, not just part of it. It's about giving Him control over your work, relationships, dreams, and struggles. When you do, you'll find a peace and purpose that no earthly achievement can offer.

The compass illustration teaches us that, as men, putting God first doesn't mean neglecting other responsibilities but putting the most effort into the areas of our lives that only we can fulfill. So much of our energy is often spent on things that anyone else could do, but there are specific roles that only you can fill. No one else can be a husband to your wife, a father to your children, or fulfill the unique purpose God has designed for you. Staying focused on Jesus is the key to fulfilling all these roles.

Hebrews 12:2 reminds us, "We do this by keeping our eyes on Jesus, the champion who initiates and perfects our faith. Because of the joy awaiting him, he endured the cross, disregarding its shame. Now he is seated in the place of honor beside God's throne." Marksmen keep their eyes on the target—Jesus—and walks in faith, casting off every weight that slows him down and the sin that tries to pull him off course. True North, in all things, is fixing your eyes on Jesus.

As we move forward in this book, remember that everything starts here. North is where we put God first, and south is where we deny ourselves. Only then can we aim for the bullseye—becoming more like Jesus.

PRACTICAL APPLICATION
SET YOUR TRUE NORTH

1) **Prayer and Journaling:** Spend some time in prayer, asking God to reveal any areas in your life where He is not first. Write down any specific areas, habits, or relationships where you sense God leading you to make changes. Be honest about any idols in your life—things you've elevated above Him.

2) **Commitment:** For the next week, choose one area where you've identified an idol or misplaced priority, and commit to reshuffling your schedule, attention, or mindset to put God first in that area. It could be your time with family, how you approach work, or your devotion time with God.

3) **Accountability:** Share this commitment with a trusted friend, pastor, or men's group. Ask them to help hold you accountable for this week and check in on your progress.

CHAPTER 2
DENY SELF

When we prioritize God, we are also called to deny ourselves, which is the next step in our journey as men of faith—represented by south on the marksmen compass. Jesus made it clear in Matthew 16:24: "If any of you wants to be my follower, you must give up your own way, take up your cross, and follow me." Denying yourself means letting go of your desires and submitting to God's will. It's not a one-time decision but a daily commitment to choose God over personal gain, comfort, or success.

True self-denial is also a matter of spiritual warfare. So much of our stumbling comes when we don't fully understand what it means to deny ourselves. Many men confuse this call and turn it into self-righteousness, making sacrifices with the wrong motives and falling into the enemy's trap. Although we may act unselfishly, we are often still torn inside because our motives aren't aligned with Christ's heart.

Authentic, healthy self-denial isn't focused on what you're giving up but on what you gain when you follow Christ. Philippians 3:7-8 says:

> *I once thought these things were valuable, but now I consider them worthless because of what Christ has done.*

> *Yes, everything else is worthless when compared with the infinite value of knowing Christ Jesus my Lord. For his sake I have discarded everything else, counting it all as garbage, so that I could gain Christ.*

This isn't about lack, self-imposed poverty, or living with a deficit; it's about enhancement—letting go of what seems valuable in exchange for something greater. When you deny yourself for Christ, you're not losing out—you're gaining infinitely more.

Bear with me as we explore this balance. Much like when you chose to follow Christ, you had to put aside your own desires. Paul tells us in Philippians 2:3-4: "Don't be selfish; don't try to impress others. Be humble, thinking of others as better than yourselves. Don't look out only for your own interests, but take an interest in others, too."

This is a tough challenge, but it's a critical step in our walk with God. Denying yourself doesn't mean diminishing who you are; it's about setting aside selfishness, the need for approval, and personal ambition to embrace humility. When you lift others above yourself, you follow Christ's example of servanthood.

Think about how to apply that. God is not asking you to give something up just for the sake of sacrifice. He's asking you to release what's holding you back from becoming more like Him, so you can live a life connected to something bigger than yourself.

How is this possible without hurting ourselves—without losing who we are in the process? Too often, men get caught up in trying to become better versions of themselves but lose sight of who God created them to be. In the pursuit of improvement, we can easily fall into the trap of perfectionism or try to meet unrealistic expectations. Instead of becoming more Christ-like, we end up burned out, frustrated, and disconnected from our true purpose.

It took me a while to understand that denying myself doesn't mean I can't be happy or enjoy life. Too many men struggle to live up to impossible standards, trying to change by sheer willpower. In the end, this often hurts them more than it helps. The Pharisees did something similar. They placed unbearable burdens on people through legalism, twisting the Law and making it harder to follow God. Matthew 23:4 tells us, "They crush people with unbearable religious demands and never lift a finger to ease the burden." They became so focused on the rules that they lost the heart of God, so much so that they couldn't even recognize Jesus when He came.

A man will lose perspective on who really matters when he isn't focused on God's direction. Even when he thinks he's doing good, he may actually be serving or hurting himself. The Bible tells us that many followed Jesus for their own personal gain. John 6:26 says, "Jesus replied, 'I tell you the truth, you want to be with me because I fed you, not because you understood the miraculous signs.'"

So, how do we avoid this pitfall? First, we must examine what the Bible teaches about self-denial and then discuss what the fruit should look like. If the end result doesn't resemble Jesus, something is off.

BIBLICAL SELF-DENIAL: REJECTING THE OLD NATURE

Biblical self-denial is not about rejecting who you are but instead rejecting your old nature, selfish ambitions, and desires that conflict with God's will for your life. Ephesians 4:22-24 says this:

Throw off your old sinful nature and your former way of life, which is corrupted by lust and deception. Instead, let the Spirit renew your thoughts and attitudes. Put on your new nature, created to be like God—truly righteous and holy.

When you do things with the wrong motive, you lose the power of the effect. It's essential to understand the difference between *self-sacrifice* and *self-denial*. Self-denial might mean giving up control to follow Jesus better, while self-sacrifice is serving others because it's your responsibility.

Reflection Question: Think about an area where you've been struggling to let go of control. What do you think might change if you genuinely handed that over to God?

THE STORY OF PETER: A JOURNEY OF SELF-DENIAL

Let's think about Peter. He followed Jesus for three years, expecting that Jesus would restore the kingdom of Israel and that Peter would be at Jesus's side when it happened. Peter had his own idea of how God's kingdom would be established. So much so that, at one point, Jesus had to correct him. In fact, Jesus even called Peter "Satan" because Peter's words echoed Satan's temptation in the wilderness—trying to throw Jesus off His path. Matthew 16:23: "Jesus turned to Peter and said, 'Get away from me, Satan! You are a dangerous trap to me. You are seeing things merely from a human point of view, not from God's.'"

Peter had been speaking through the Spirit earlier, and Jesus said he was blessed because he did not hear from just a human being (Matthew 16:17). Then, suddenly, Peter became a mouthpiece for Satan's deception. Peter was following Jesus, but was he genuinely denying himself, or was he seeking something more for himself?

When the pressure was on, Peter publicly denied Jesus three times. Matthew 26:74-75 recounts Peter's denial: Peter swore, "A curse on me if I'm lying—I don't know the man!" And immediately, the rooster crowed.

> *Suddenly, Jesus' words flashed through Peter's mind: "Before the rooster crows, you will deny three times that you even know me." And he went away, weeping bitterly.*

This is what happens when we don't deny ourselves. A self-centered man can follow Christ only for so long before he goes into survival mode in a moment of trouble or persecution and denies Christ, choosing himself first. Though he was close to Jesus, Peter struggled with self-denial—just as we all do.

It took Peter a while to indeed die to self. Men need to understand this: the process of dying to our flesh is not easy. Some would argue that Peter was closer to Jesus than anyone. Yet, he did not fully grasp self-denial until Jesus returned. When Peter saw Him again, he ran to Jesus on the shore, where Jesus taught him one of the most critical lessons on self-denial in the entire Bible. I'll pause here as a teaser and revisit this later.

SELF-DENIAL OR SELF-RIGHTEOUSNESS?

In my early days of Christian zeal, I didn't know the difference between a personal conviction and the teachings of Christ. I didn't understand the process of *sanctification*—the journey of transformation that takes time as people grow. I wasn't patient with other people in different stages of their lives, each struggling with unique things.

I went to church, where some people had strict rules. I'm not here to argue right or wrong, but I want you to understand the truth about self-denial. I was being taught a list of "dos and don'ts." While some people need rules in black and white for structure, I needed to know *why*. I do better when I understand the "why" behind something rather than just how; when I know the *why*, I'm more motivated to follow through on the *how*.

I'll admit I have a rebellious nature—tell me I can't do something, and I'll do the opposite, sometimes out of spite. So, I worked the system to fit my rebellious nature—I adapted any proposed rule to fit my desires without understanding the purpose and heart behind them, thinking I would become a better version of myself. At the time, two rules that stuck out to me in my youth group were no rated-R movies and no secular music. Now, the music thing didn't bother me much, but the movies? That was a tough one for me to give up because I am a movie buff, so naturally, I chose to strongly enforce the music rule but ignored the movie rule—that one would cost too much. This conviction to renounce secular music did not come from me—I was given two choices, so I chose the one that seemed most feasible and convinced myself that enforcing the rule with an iron fist made me more like Jesus.

One day, I came home to find my roommate's cousin using my stereo to play his secular rock music. Feeling like I had the righteousness of God on my side, I turned off his "devil's music" and told him why it was wrong. I look back now and wonder—what did I think I was going to accomplish? Was I concerned about him, or was I trying to show off my own pride in my self-denial of secular music?

This young man had left the faith because of the judgment he'd faced from Christians, and here I was, making my witness about music instead of Christ. I'll never forget what he said to me that day. He asked, "What's the difference between the music I'm listening to and the movies you're watching?" He knew us and knew we had just gone to the movies over the weekend, and yes, the movie was rated R.

That hit me hard. I realized my self-denial wasn't about Jesus or His love for people—it was about me trying to be better. Cutting things out of your life is necessary and reasonable, but my motives were off. Instead of being like Jesus, who met the woman at the well and had a life-changing conversation with her while she was still struggling, I was more like the Pharisees, angry that Jesus sat with sinners: When the Pharisees saw this, they asked his disciples, "Why does your teacher eat with such scum?"

> When Jesus heard this, he said, "Healthy people don't need a doctor—sick people do." Then he added, "Now go and learn the meaning of this Scripture: 'I want you to show mercy, not offer sacrifices.' For I have come to call not those who think they are righteous, but those who know they are sinners." —Matthew 9:11-13

I wasn't trying to be like Jesus—I was just trying to be better than I was in an area that was easy for me to give up. That will only take you so far, and it won't produce the kind of fruit that inspires or changes others. These are not the kind of changes we are to make—just following rules without allowing God to change our hearts. In this verse, we see Jesus's primary motivation stems from the love in His heart for us. Now, I want things cut out of my life not because I want approval or to be seen as a good Christian. I want God to change my heart. It was never about music or movies; it was about learning how to walk differently and purify my heart. When we do things out of obligation, we become more like the Pharisees and less like Jesus.

Often, this kind of self-denial can lead to bitterness. We become angry at others for doing things we secretly still want to do. Psalm 73:3 says, "For I envied the proud when I saw them prosper despite their wickedness." We forget that self-denial isn't about following rules for the sake of it; it's about drawing closer to Jesus and letting Him transform our hearts.

PRACTICAL STEPS TOWARD SELF-DENIAL

1) **Daily Surrender**
   Denying yourself is a daily practice. Every day, ask yourself, What part of my life am I holding back from God?
2) **Listen to God's Will**
   Ask God what He desires for you today. Be willing to submit to His plan, even when it doesn't align with your own desires.
3) **Follow the Perfect Model**

Key Verse: "You must have the same attitude that Christ Jesus had. Though he was God, he did not think of equality with God as something to cling to. Instead, he gave up his divine privileges; he took the humble position of a slave and was born as a human being" (Philippians 2:5-7).

THE LESSON OF TRUE SELF-DENIAL

Now, let's get back to Peter. He had to live with the reality that, despite all his bold claims, he denied Jesus in public. But thank God, Peter didn't have to stay in that shame. Jesus gave him the chance to make it right. Honestly, I'm so grateful that God provides us with the opportunity to fix our mistakes. He doesn't leave us drowning in guilt or regret. We can get it right by doing what's right.

> **No matter how far off track we've gotten, there's always a way back to Jesus if we're willing to run toward Him.**

So, when Peter saw Jesus again, he didn't waste any time. He literally jumped out of the boat and ran straight to Him. I love that picture because it shows how much Peter still wanted to be close to Jesus, even after messing up. And that's key for all of us: no matter how far off track we've gotten, there's always a way back to Jesus if we're willing to run toward Him.

In John 21, something powerful happens after Peter's desperate reunion with Jesus. Jesus asks Peter three times if he loves Him—probably to match the three times Peter denied Him. Then He tells Peter to "feed His sheep," which was a way of saying, "Take care of my people." Jesus is giving Peter the responsibility to lead and serve. But here's the part that really hits home. In John 21:18-19, Jesus says:

> *"I tell you the truth, when you were young, you were able to do as you liked; you dressed yourself and went wherever you wanted to go. But when you are old, you will stretch out your hands, and others will dress you and take you where you don't want to go."*

This passage was about more than just getting older. Jesus was telling Peter what kind of death he would face for following Him. Peter, the same guy who denied Jesus out of fear, was now going to live and die for the gospel. Jesus was saying, "You're not in control anymore. Following Me is going to take you places you never thought you'd go—and it's going to cost you."

I remember reading this as a teenager and thinking, *Hold on, I'm young, and I don't get to do what I want.* But as I got older, I realized that Jesus was talking about more than just physical age. He was talking about spiritual maturity. A mature man doesn't just follow his own desires; he lets God lead him, even when it's hard—even when he's not in control.

After Jesus drops this heavy truth on Peter, Peter does what many men do when things get uncomfortable—he looks for a way to shift the focus. Peter glances over at John and says, *"What about him?"*

What God has for you is different from what He has for someone else.

I get it. Jesus had just told Peter that following Him was going to cost him his life, and Peter was like, *"Okay, but what about that* guy? Does he have to go through this, too?" And Jesus hits him with a powerful truth: "If I want him to remain alive until I return, what is that to you? As for you, follow me." (John 21:22).

Here's the lesson: *comparison kills calling*. What God has for you is different from what He has for someone else. Peter's calling was going to cost him everything, but John's path was different. And Jesus is saying, *"Don't worry about him. You need to focus on what I've called you to do."*

This statement is the key to true self-denial. It's not about comparing yourself to others or trying to live up to someone else's journey. Denying yourself is personal—it's about following Jesus in the unique way He's called you to and looking to God's Word to define your path for you. Peter had to accept that his path was his own, and so do we.

When we start comparing our calling to someone else's, we lose focus. It's not about living up to a set of rules or trying to be better than someone else. It's about surrendering our hearts to God and letting Him lead us on our path. Jesus was showing Peter that denying yourself isn't just about sacrifice—it's about obedience and trusting God's plan for your life, no matter how it looks compared to someone else's.

THE ROOT OF SELF-DENIAL

We must also realize that true self-denial is rooted in God's standard, not our own. As men, we might be tempted to redefine what a "man of God" looks like, adjusting the standards to fit our desires or the expectations of the world around us. But God has already set the example through His Son, Jesus, and given us His Word as our foundation.

Paul warned in 2 Timothy 3:5 (NIV) about people "having a form of godliness but denying its power." This passage warns us of what happens when we try to create our own standards and ignore God's. We may think we're living righteously, but without the power of Christ in our lives and hearts, we're just going through the motions.

True self-denial is about conforming to the image of Christ, as Romans 8:29 reminds us: "For God knew his people in advance, and he chose them to become like his Son so that his Son would be the firstborn among many brothers and sisters."

Our goal of self-denial is not to meet our own standards or the world's but to reflect on Jesus more each day. Jesus set the ultimate example of humility and sacrifice, and we are called to follow in His footsteps. Philippians 2:5-7 says clearly: "You must have the same attitude that Christ Jesus had. Though he was God, he did not think of equality with God as something to cling to. Instead, he gave up his divine privileges; he took the humble position of a slave and was born as a human being."

God is holy, gracious, and merciful; in denying ourselves, we align our lives with His character. We cannot make up our own version of godliness. Everything will ultimately be held to the standard of God's original, sinless creation. While none of us can match that perfection, we are called to strive toward it. Paul understood this struggle, which is why he shared in Philippians 3:12-14:

> *I don't mean to say that I have already achieved these things or that I have already reached perfection. But I press on to possess that perfection for which Christ Jesus first possessed me. No, dear brothers and sisters, I have*

not achieved it, but I focus on this one thing: Forgetting the past and looking forward to what lies ahead, I press on to reach the end of the race and receive the heavenly prize for which God, through Christ Jesus, is calling us.

As marksmen of faith, we may not always hit the bullseye, but we continue to aim for it because our standard is Jesus.

Denying ourselves means trusting that God's plan is better than our own, even when it's hard and costs us something valuable. The reward is not just in what we give up but in what we gain: a closer walk with Christ, a life lived according to His will, and a heart conformed to His image. Jesus is still, and always will be, the standard.

PRACTICAL APPLICATION
STEPS TOWARD DAILY SELF-DENIAL

Self-denial is not a one-time action but a daily discipline that requires intentional effort. Here are a few steps to help you put self-denial into practice:

1) **Daily Surrender in Prayer:** Each morning, take a few minutes to ask God to help you surrender your desires and plans for the day. Ask for strength to submit to His will in your decisions and interactions, no matter how small they seem. A simple prayer might be: "Lord, help me to deny myself today. Lead me in Your ways and give me the strength to follow where You guide, even when it's difficult."

2) **Identify One Area to Let Go:** Take a close look at your life and identify one area where you may be holding onto control. It could be a habit, a relationship, or a personal goal that may not align with God's will. Commit this area

to Him. Write it down and ask God to help you release it in His timing.

3) **Serve Others in a Small Way:** Each day, find one opportunity to put someone else's needs above your own. Whether at home, work, or in your community, look for a way to serve selflessly. It could be as simple as lending a listening ear, offering help to someone in need, or going out of your way to show kindness.

4) **Reflect on Progress:** At the end of the day, reflect on moments when you practiced self-denial. Where did you succeed, and where did you struggle? This isn't about condemnation—it's about growth. Ask God to help you grow stronger in those areas where you struggled and give thanks for the victories.

5) **Read and Meditate on Philippians 2:5-7:** Take time to read this passage and meditate on how Jesus denied Himself to serve others. Let this example inspire your actions. Ask God to give you the mindset of Christ in your own life, so you can serve with humility and obedience.

CHAPTER 3

PART A: VALUE FAMILY

East represents valuing family. Our first ministry begins at home, where we are called to lead by example as husbands, fathers, brothers, and sons. Valuing family means not only leading our own households but also showing respect and honor to our parents and elders, loving our siblings, and passing on a legacy of faith through generations.

From the very beginning of creation, the man was given the responsibility of the family. Genesis 2:15 says, "The LORD God placed the man in the Garden of Eden to tend and watch over it." Everything in the garden was entrusted to Adam's care, and by extension, Eve as well. God's design for the household placed man in leadership. However, as we can see, Adam could have fulfilled that role better. Instead of protecting his wife and guarding the garden, he allowed the serpent to deceive Eve, leading to their downfall. When confronted by God, Adam didn't take responsibility. In Genesis 3:12, Adam replied, "It was the woman you gave me who gave me the fruit, and I ate it." Here, Adam not only blamed his wife but indirectly blamed God.

When men neglect their calling to lead, protect, and love their families, it leaves room for rebellion against God's Word. It becomes an opening for the enemy or even our own sin nature to twist God's Word into something that sounds justified but ultimately leads to rebellion. This is precisely what the serpent did in the garden—he twisted God's words, making it appear as though they didn't mean what Adam and Eve had understood them to mean. "Did God really say you must not eat the fruit from any tree in the garden?" (Genesis 3:1). A man's failure to lead spiritually opens the door to confusion and division.

As men, our families are under our care, and we must value this fantastic responsibility. Though we may shy away from words like work, commitment, or accountability, these are the cornerstones of building the type of family we are called to establish. We must become the fathers, husbands, sons, and brothers God intends for us to be, and the only way we can is by relying on the strength that God provides.

THE ROLE OF A SON

The Bible clearly teaches that we are to honor our father and mother as sons. This scripture is not a suggestion but a commandment tied directly to a promise:

> "Honor your father and mother." This is the first commandment with a promise: If you honor your father and mother, "things will go well for you, and you will have a long life on the earth." —Ephesians 6:2-3

Notice that the verse doesn't add conditions like "only if your parents are honorable." It simply commands us to honor them.

I grew up in a home where it was challenging to show honor to my parents. But as I matured, I realized that honoring my parents was less about them and more about honoring God. I honored them because God's Word tells me to, and in doing so, I honored Him.

Reflection Question: What does honoring your parents look like in your life today, even if it's difficult?

THE ROLE OF A HUSBAND

The Bible tells us to love our wives in the same way that Christ loves the church. Ephesians 5:25 says, "For husbands, this means love your wives, just as Christ loved the church. He gave up his life for her." While many men love to emphasize that wives should submit to their husbands, the real challenge is directed at the men. We are called to love our wives sacrificially. The kind of love we are called to express is not domineering but Christ-like—a love that serves and sacrifices.

This responsibility is crucial because how we lead and care for our families directly impacts our relationship with God. As husbands, the way we treat our wives doesn't just affect our marriages—it can strengthen or weaken our connection with God Himself.

First Peter 3:7 says, "In the same way, you husbands must give honor to your wives. Treat your wife with understanding as you live together. She may be weaker than you are, but she is your equal partner in God's gift of new life. Treat her as you should so your prayers will not be hindered." This verse emphasizes that neglecting our responsibilities at home directly impacts our spiritual life and can hinder our prayers.

Don't get this verse twisted—it's not easy to live out. Understanding women is challenging, and men often misunderstand what Peter means when he says women are "weaker." It's not just about physical weakness. The word "weaker" here can also refer to the different strengths that men and women possess. Women are incredibly strong in many ways, especially emotionally and spiritually. As husbands, we must recognize that our roles may differ, but they are not lesser.

Equality here does not mean equal in responsibility or even in function—it means we are both equally vital to God's plan. In a marriage, both husband and wife are essential to raising the next generation and creating a home that reflects Christ. Ephesians 5:31 reinforces this by saying, "As the Scriptures say, 'A man leaves his father and mother and is joined to his wife, and the two are united into one.'"

This unity is impossible without mutual honor, respect, and love. I genuinely hope you reflect on the meaning of this verse. It calls us as husbands to go beyond merely coexisting with our wives; it challenges us to understand them, honor them, and work alongside them as equal partners in the eyes of God. When we do this, we not only strengthen our marriages but also open the door for God's blessings in our spiritual lives.

Reflection Question: How does your love for your wife reflect the sacrificial love Christ has for the church?

THE ROLE OF A FATHER

As fathers, we are called to raise our children in the ways of the Lord. Proverbs 22:6 teaches, "Direct your children onto the right path, and when they are older, they will not leave it." The enemy works hard to break up families because he knows the power of a strong, united household. Studies show that children raised without a father are more likely to experience behavioral problems, drop out of school, and face emotional and psychological challenges. In fact, research indicates that "children raised in fatherless homes are four times more likely to live in poverty and are more likely to drop out of school."[1] Fatherhood is more than providing financially or being present physically. It's being emotionally and spiritually available. It's about spiritual guidance, emotional support, and being a godly example. When we take our responsibility seriously, we set our children up for success—not just in the world but in their walk with God.

Reflection Question: How are you intentionally guiding your children toward Christ in their daily lives?

THE ROLE OF A BROTHER

Being a brother or sibling extends beyond blood relationships. As part of the family of God, we are called to bear one another's burdens and lift each other up. Galatians 6:2 says, "Share each other's burdens, and in this way obey the law of Christ." In the same way that we support our blood brothers and sisters, we are to encourage and care for our brothers and sisters in Christ. James 5:16 urges us, "Confess your sins to each other and pray for each other so that you may be healed. The earnest prayer of a righteous person has great power and produces wonderful results."

---

[1] Jack Brewer, *Fatherlessness in Florida*, (America First Policy Institute, December 29, 2024), https://americafirstpolicy.com/issues/fatherlessness-in-florida.

True brotherhood in Christ means we step in when others are weak, we share in their struggles, and we help carry their burdens. As men, we must be accountable to each other, supporting one another not only in times of strength but also in times of weakness.

Reflection Question: How can you be a better brother in Christ to those around you?

PERSONAL EXPERIENCES

This feels like a lot, and that's because it is. There's no escaping the weight of responsibility as Marksmen, as a man of faith, as a man of God—the value of family.

> **There is no higher calling for a man than to be about his family and God's extended family.**

When you really think about it and let it sink deep into your heart, what greater calling could we have? What more significant achievement is there than creating new life—and not just making it but raising it in a way that leads into the eternal presence of God? What greater miracle is there than God using you to lead your family, a brother, or even a stranger into a right relationship with Him through Jesus?

There is no higher calling for a man than to be about his family and God's extended family.

This was a struggle for me because my view of family was twisted. My understanding of family was distorted. I won't dive into a list of all the traumas I dealt with, but let me give you some perspective. I didn't grow up in a traditional family situation. I saw and experienced things at a young age that impacted me for my entire life. The hurt in my family tree is hard to describe, full of traumatic events—things I repressed and tried to forget, with situations etched in my mind that shaped my adulthood. These events happened when I was still a child and followed me into adulthood.

I know I didn't have it completely bad. My grandparents on my mom's side were good people who tried to show us a better way, but they passed when I was young. My mom was loving and supportive, but we were all impacted by my dad's issues—his drug abuse, being in and out of jail his whole life, and his anger issues dominated the culture of our household. As a teenager, I directly followed in his footsteps with the same destructive patterns. His absence and inability to deal with his own past created a void in my family that the enemy was able to exploit.

Men, I say this as someone who could swap sob stories with the best of them, but hear me when I say that none of that matters once we become new creations in Christ. We must break the cycle, process the hurt, and become men of character who love, cherish, and lead our families. We can't run from this responsibility. No matter how much it hurts, we must ask God for help and follow His Word on what our homes should look like.

Even today, I carry regrets, guilt, and shame for the mistakes I've made. I got married with unresolved issues, even as a Christian. I brought a lot of baggage. I married young and stepped into a family, taking on kids who weren't biologically mine, but I wanted to lead and love them like they were. I'm grateful they call me "Dad," and I'm thankful we're good now, but I made a lot of mistakes early on. Like many men, I didn't have the correct view of family life. I didn't know how to process my feelings or how to ask for help.

Nothing I'm saying is easy, but you must value your role in your family. I thank God I've learned how to forgive and how to ask for forgiveness. I know now that it's okay to be weak, to talk to my mentors, and to open up about my struggles. That's normal. Who is really equipped to be a father? I had three kids before I ever held a newborn of my own. It wasn't until that moment *that* I realized what God had placed in my hands, holding my youngest and seeing his first breaths.

Nothing else in this world means more than family. This is why the world, its system, and its culture try to downplay the role of family, making everything about self—your feelings, your happiness. But as men of God, we must find joy in being family men, in whatever capacity that may be. Even if you never become a biological father, you are still called to mentor, to lead, and to invest in the next generation. Even if you never become a husband, you love to protect women; even if your parents abandoned you, honor your elders and those who came before you. No matter your situation, family matters.

THE FAMILY DESIGN

Family, as designed by God, mirrors the deep intimacy and connection He longs to have with each of us. Every layer of human relationship—whether it's being a spouse, a parent, or a sibling—gives us a glimpse of how God relates to us. This is the kind of closeness He desires from us, not just as Creator to creation but as intimate family.

God calls Himself the Bridegroom, and we are His bride. Think about that for a second—He's not just after some distant relationship but a love and commitment like the deepest marriage bond. John 3:29 (NIV) says, "The bride belongs to the bridegroom. The friend who attends the bridegroom waits and listens for him, and is full of joy when he hears the bridegroom's voice." God's love for us is that committed, that devoted. The bond of marriage was always meant to reflect His relationship with us. Ephesians 5:25 lays it out clearly: "For husbands, this means love your wives, just as Christ loved the church. He gave up his life for her to make her holy and clean." Christ's sacrificial love is the model for our own relationships, especially within our families.

But it's not just the picture of a marriage. God is also a friend who sticks closer than a brother. Proverbs 18:24 says, "There are 'friends' who destroy each other, but a real friend sticks closer than a brother." He isn't some distant deity watching from above. No, He's that loyal friend, always faithful, never leaving. This isn't just head knowledge—this is the heart of God, committed and present even when others fall away.

He is our leader—our example—yet He doesn't just call us servants or followers, but friends. John 15:15 says, "I no longer call you slaves because a master doesn't confide in his slaves. Now you are my friends since I have told you everything the Father told me." This isn't about following rules or orders—it's about intimacy and trust. He's opened His heart to us, revealing His plans and His will and inviting us into a relationship built on closeness.

Then comes the most personal level of all—God calls us sons and daughters. We're not just His creation; we're His children. Second Corinthians 6:18 says, "I will be your Father, and you will be my sons and daughters." When we come into His family, we gain more than just a distant relationship with God—we become His own. This means we can approach Him not just as the Almighty but as our loving *Abba* (Romans 8:15). *Abba* means "Daddy" in Aramaic and reflects a deep personal connection.

But here's something we've got to understand: we're not born into God's family by natural means. This is key. John 1:12 explains it like this: "But to all who believed him and accepted him, he gave the right to become children of God." It's through belief in Christ that we become sons and daughters of God. It's not automatic. Yes, every person is created in the image of God (Genesis 1:27), but it's only through Christ that we gain the right to be His children.

> **The same sacrificial love Christ showed for us on the cross is the love we are called to show for our families.**

This is why Paul says in Romans 8:15 that we receive the "Spirit of adoption" through Christ. We aren't God's children by birthright but by choice—His choice. I get this on a personal level because I've adopted children. They weren't born into my family, but I chose them. I brought them in, and they became my own. There's a beauty in being chosen, in being wanted. Galatians 4:5 sums it up perfectly: "God sent him to buy freedom for us who were slaves to the law, so that he could adopt us as his very own children." God chose you; He paid for you, and He redeemed you to be His own. That's how much family matters to God.

The high price God paid to make us part of His family should change how we look at our own families. As men, we're called to lead our families with that same dedication and sacrifice. Just as Christ is the head of the church, you are called to be the head of your home (Ephesians 5:23). It's not easy. It requires sacrifice, responsibility, and a heart that's always pointing toward God's design for the family.

God's example of family is the foundation for how we're called to live as husbands, fathers, and brothers. The same sacrificial love Christ showed for us on the cross is the love we are called to show for our families. God's design for family is not just about blood—it's about a relationship founded on love, commitment, and sacrifice. Men, don't underestimate the calling you have. Value your family the way God values you. It's worth the cost.

CHAPTER 4

WEST PART B: UPHOLD MINISTRY

East and West are deeply connected. Both represent responsibilities that, if we don't see how they intertwine, can end up hindering one another. I've seen men get so focused on ministry that they neglect their families. And I've also seen men use family as an excuse to never engage in ministry.

Think of it like the lines on a compass. While keeping God first as our True North should always be our focus, we should also balance responsibilities at home (East) and in ministry (West). These areas aren't in competition. Your home is your first ministry, but the advancement of the gospel and making disciples is also a critical calling and your responsibility. Both are vital because your first disciples will be in your home. It's crucial to stay balanced. When we focus too much on one and neglect the other, we risk losing sight of our mission and our purpose.

When we talk about "upholding ministry," we're continuing the work Christ gave us to do—loving and leading our families and continuing the mission of the church. Ministry means to serve others in the name of Christ. It's how we fulfill our calling by spreading the gospel, caring for the needs of others, and teaching them to grow spiritually. It involves leadership, teaching, discipleship, and support, whether formally as pastors or deacons or informally in everyday life. Ministry is about embodying Christ's love and serving both the church community and those in the world around us.

Mark 10:45 gives us the heart of ministry: "For even the Son of Man came not to be served but to serve others and to give his life as a ransom for many." Ministry, then, is about putting others' needs ahead of our own and following Christ's example of servant leadership.

Reflection Question: Are you serving your family and church with a Christ-like heart of service?

THE HEART OF MINISTRY

Jesus demonstrated what ministry truly is: serving others. James 1:27 tells us that "pure and genuine religion in the sight of God the Father means caring for orphans and widows in their distress and refusing to let the world corrupt you." Here, James points us to what true worship and ministry look like—taking care of those most in need, especially those who have nothing to give in return. Ministry isn't about what we gain or the recognition we receive; it's about glorifying God through service. And nothing that Jesus asks of us is something He didn't model Himself, as we read in Mark 10:45. However, ministry can quickly become distorted when it's focused on self-promotion—when it becomes about achievement, recognition, or advancement rather than serving others and bringing glory to God. The Bible warns us about people who preach the gospel for their own personal gain. Philippians 1:17 cautions, "Those others do not have pure motives as they preach about Christ. They preach with selfish ambition, not sincerely, intending to make my chains more painful to me." Paul is describing those who preach for selfish reasons, seeking to promote themselves rather than the gospel of Christ. This is a reminder that not everyone in ministry has the right motives, which is why we must constantly examine our hearts and stay aligned with God's purpose.

> **We need to be careful not to let our expectations of recognition define our fulfillment.**

Jesus Himself warns against such behavior in Matthew 6:1, saying, "Watch out! Don't do your good deeds publicly, to be admired by others, for you will lose the reward from your Father in heaven." He reminds us that when we seek attention and approval from others, instead of doing things quietly for God's glory, we lose sight of the actual reward—God's approval.

Ministry should be life-giving but only when Christ is at the center. It feels good to help others, and it fills us with a sense of purpose. But we need to be careful not to let our expectations of recognition define our fulfillment. Jesus taught that service is meant to glorify God, not ourselves. If we're doing ministry or serving our families for the sake of recognition or what we hope to get in return, we're setting ourselves up for disappointment. Both in family life and in ministry, our focus should be on giving and serving without expecting anything in return, just as Christ gave Himself entirely for us.

A LESSON FROM CHRISTMAS

Let me share a simple example. One Christmas, I went all out and bought a gift for my niece that I thought would absolutely blow her away. I was excited to see her reaction, expecting her to light up with joy. But when I gave it to her, she barely reacted—just a little smirk, far from the excitement I had anticipated. At that moment, I could have felt disappointed or even frustrated. But I had to stop and check myself. Was I giving that gift to her, or was I doing it for me? Was I hoping for my own sense of fulfillment, or was my focus indeed on blessing her? Maybe it was a little of both, but here's the lesson: true love means giving even when you don't get the response you were hoping for.

Jesus teaches us in Luke 6:32, "If you love only those who love you, why should you get credit for that? Even sinners love those who love them!" Ministry isn't about how others respond; it's about staying faithful to what God has called us to do. Whether it's giving gifts, serving in ministry, or loving those who don't love us back, we are called to act from a place of selfless love, not based on the reaction we receive.

I can share countless stories where I didn't get the response I expected. I've been attacked, lied about, and faced many hurtful things, even when I was doing my best to do what was right. I've been criticized and mocked, yet God has always given me the insight to move forward. He's taught me how to guard my heart because even He, in His perfection, was not always welcomed with open arms and acceptance.

If God responded to us based on how we reacted or what we deserved, we'd all be in trouble. Thank God He models a love that isn't conditional on our reactions but is grounded in His grace.

Jesus's life wasn't spared from hardship, but He has the Holy Spirit to endure it, just as we have in relationship with him. We are called to love and serve, regardless of the outcomes, trusting that God sees the heart and will reward faithfulness.

Reflection Questions:
- Have you ever done something for someone and felt disappointed by their response? How did it make you feel, and how did you handle it?
- In what ways can you practice giving or serving without expecting anything in return?
- How can you guard your heart from becoming discouraged when your efforts in ministry or life aren't met with the reaction you hoped for?

MINISTRY AND FAMILY IN BALANCE

Ministry can't be about your personal fulfillment—it needs to be connected directly to the fulfillment we find in Christ. Every believer's journey starts somewhere, and we all feel joy when we're part of something meaningful. Being part of a church team or serving others brings a sense of belonging. But we can't base our value on how others receive what we do. There will be times when you feel like you're doing everything right, but the results don't match your expectations.

Upholding the ministry of Jesus means persevering through those moments. No matter how hard it gets, you don't quit. Ministry isn't about recognition or visible results—it's about faithfulness.

Now, ministry and family are closely tied together. According to Paul, a man cannot effectively lead in the church if he does not first manage his family well. First Timothy 3:4-5 says, "He must manage his own family well, having children who respect and obey him. For if a man cannot manage his own household, how can he take care of God's church?" This doesn't mean a perfect family, but it does mean that family is your first ministry. It also doesn't mean you should neglect ministry when things are difficult at home. Balance means asking God for help and finding the strength to lead in both areas.

BREAKING THE HABIT OF AVOIDING MINISTRY

I want to break the habit that I've seen in many men who see ministry as conflicting with family life, especially when things get tough. What I've found is that men often view ministry as something they'll do later or when things settle down. But in my experience, if we wait for the perfect moment, it never comes.

I've seen faithful single women who work hard, raise their children, and still find time to serve in ministry. They press in when life gets overwhelming. They call prayer meetings. They show up. And yes, I've seen men who do this, too, but more often than not, I find men stepping back from ministry when life gets hard.

SEEKING GREATNESS IN SERVANTHOOD

Let's break that cycle. Balance isn't swinging from one extreme to another; it's staying grounded, facing challenges head-on, and looking to God for strength.

I'm a big sports fan, and I've always admired the greatness of athletes. Stephen Curry is the greatest shooter ever. But I grew up in the Jordan era, and to me, Michael Jordan is the G.O.A.T. My sons argue for LeBron James, and that debate will probably continue for a long time in our house. We all measure greatness differently—how many titles, MVPs, and scoring records. But in the kingdom of God, greatness is measured by something completely different. Jesus said in Luke 22:26, "But among you it will be different. Those who are the greatest among you should take the lowest rank, and the leader should be like a servant."

True greatness is found in servanthood, both in your home and in the church. There are no small jobs in the kingdom. Matthew 10:42 says, "And if you give even a cup of cold water to one of the least of my followers, you will surely be rewarded." Even the smallest act done for God's glory has excellent value. So, don't let an undisciplined life keep you from fulfilling the calling God has placed on you.

Family and ministry are not separate—they are interconnected. To uphold the ministry of Christ means we must serve both at home and in the church. Let's be men who rise to this call, not shrinking back when life gets hard but pressing in with strength, balance, and a heart to serve.

PRACTICAL APPLICATION
VALUE BOTH FAMILY AND MINISTRY

1) **Daily Surrender:** Take time each day to ask God how you can balance your responsibilities at home and in ministry. Pray for wisdom to serve with humility.
2) **Intentional Service:** Whether in your family or church, commit to one act of service this week that is completely selfless—where you expect nothing in return.
3) **Accountability:** Partner with a trusted friend or mentor and check in regularly on how you're balancing family and ministry. Ask for prayer when needed.

PART 2

THE MEASURE OF A MARKSMAN

Now that we've covered what it looks like to walk in the way of the marksmen, we'll dive into the steps it takes to live it out. The phrase "the measure of a man" refers to the standard by which a person's true character, integrity, and worth are evaluated. Taking measurements of who you are is a crucial process for every man—to take an honest look at himself and consider who he truly is on the inside. So often, our identity is wrapped up in what we do rather than who we are. But when a man understands who he is and knows the standard he's striving for, he can live his life with precision and purpose.

Like aiming for a bullseye, hitting the mark means striving to be more like Jesus in every area of our lives. Paul said it well in Philippians 3:12 and 14:

> *I don't mean to say that I have already achieved these things or that I have already reached perfection. But I press on to possess that perfection for which Christ Jesus first possessed me. . . . I press on to reach the end*

> *of the race and receive the heavenly prize. The journey of becoming the man God has called us to be is about pressing forward. You won't aim for perfection in a single moment, but you will grow closer to Christ and His example more regularly.*

The "measure of a marksman" is found in the growth process, illustrated as a target, with each ring representing a different challenge. Like a target, each step inward brings us closer to the bullseye—becoming more like Jesus. Each ring is more complex to hit, representing the increasing challenges of growing in our faith and character. These areas challenge us to grow as men of faith and act as milestones for measuring ourselves.

The five stages of growth are:

1) The Fear of God—The outer ring and the first steps. This is where the journey begins.
2) Knowing the Word—The next ring and the essential step for all men to follow.
3) Maturing as Men—The middle ring and the place where most men struggle. This is about moving beyond the basics and becoming men of maturity who make wise decisions and take responsibility.
4) Knowing Who You Are—The inner ring is where many men quit. Understanding your identity in Christ is crucial.
5) Becoming More Like Jesus—The bullseye. The ultimate goal is Christ-likeness.

In the chapters ahead, we'll explore each of these stages in depth. We'll understand what they mean, how to apply them to our lives, and how to measure where we stand. True marksmen not only know where they are going but also understand the process and what it takes to get there.

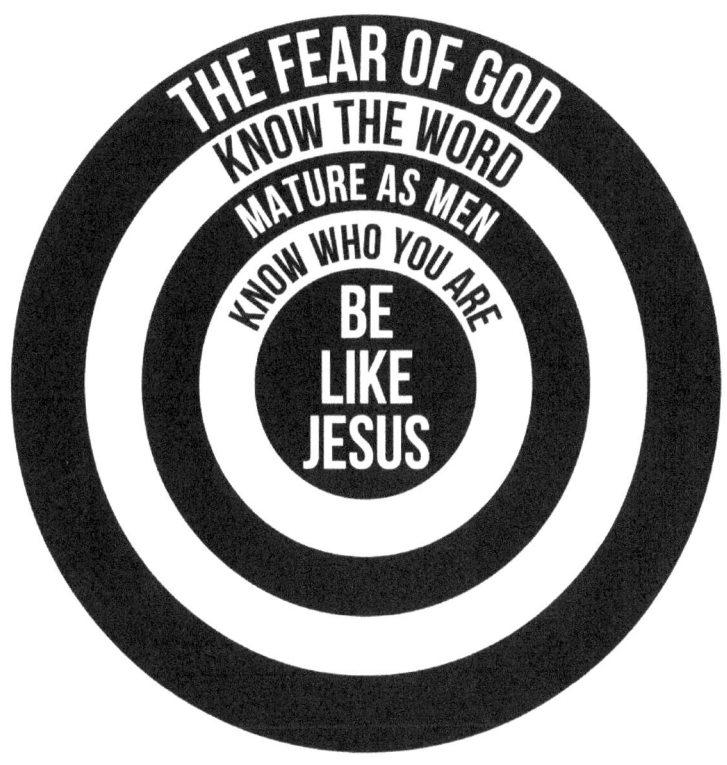

CHAPTER 5
THE FEAR OF GOD

When you look at the marksmen target, the fear of God is the outer ring—the starting point.

Proverbs 9:10 says, "Fear of the LORD is the foundation of wisdom."

It all begins with a deep respect for God, and this reverence is the cornerstone of becoming a Christian and a disciple.

The path to going deeper in our relationship with God takes new life when we truly understand the One we are on this journey with. Many men, myself included, can sometimes take for granted the calling and responsibility we have to know and represent God on a deeper personal level. If we're not careful, we might approach our relationship with God lightly, downplaying the significance of who He is in our lives. Handling our responsibilities or relationships carelessly can cause them to lose meaning and purpose, especially when we put in half the effort without concern for the consequences or the intention behind our actions.

A healthy fear of or reverence for God realigns us with a deeper purpose and a higher calling as we pay more attention to detail in our approach. When you genuinely care about something and hold it in reverence, you take better care of it. As insignificant as this example may seem, it's the best I can offer because I struggle to find the words to capture how important it is to revere God.

I love cars. I would always buy a new car if it weren't such a poor financial decision. When I first get that new car, I'm mindful of everything. I don't allow food in the car, and I'll park miles away to avoid door dings. I'm almost obsessed with ensuring nothing happens to the car—I revere it. But as time goes on and the car gets older, I start to care less. A scratch here, a ding there—it doesn't bother me as much anymore. I begin to take the car for granted.

> **The fear of God starts us on this journey, and once we lose it, we will miss the target entirely.**

If we're not careful, this can happen in our view of God. We lose that initial reverence, that holy fear that changes our view of our relationship with Him. Over time, our awareness of His greatness fades, and we begin to handle our faith with less care and urgency.

We can't afford to let that happen. The fear of God is meant to keep us aligned, to remind us of His holiness and our need for Him in every part of our lives. Just like a car, if we neglect proper care and attention, we risk losing the deeper connection and purpose that comes with reverence. The fear of God starts us on this journey, and once we lose it, we will miss the target entirely.

DEFINING FEAR

The "fear" we're discussing here isn't the typical fear that makes us want to run away. It's awe, reverence, and an understanding of who God is. When we grasp His power, holiness, and overwhelming love for us, it reshapes how we live. Our decisions start to honor Him, and we begin to place Him at the center of everything we do.

In the marksmen target, the fear of God is represented first because anyone who truly understands who God is should have a healthy reverence for Him. That is a good starting place.

Jesus even said in Matthew 10:28 (author paraphrase), "Don't fear those who can kill the body; rather, fear the one who can destroy both body and soul in hell." At first glance, that seems like a harsh teaching, but Jesus emphasizes the stakes of whom we worship.

So, let's unpack this. Jesus tells us not to fear those who can only harm us physically. The body, after all, is temporary. We live in a broken world, and danger, persecution, or even death are real possibilities for following Christ. But Jesus says, "That's not where the ultimate danger lies." The body is essential, but our souls—our eternal selves—are what truly matter. And only God holds the power over both.

This verse doesn't suggest that God is waiting to condemn us but to show us His authority. The fear Jesus speaks of here is a deep awareness of God's sovereignty over our eternal destiny.

It's about understanding the weight of eternity and who truly controls it. Fearing God in this way isn't about being terrified of punishment but about recognizing that the same God who has the power to judge is also the One who has the power to save. He loves us beyond comprehension.

What Jesus is getting at is this: the stakes are eternal. The people around us, those who may threaten or hurt us, only have temporary power. But God's power is eternal. He has authority over life beyond this world. Fearing Him, in the way Jesus means, is about putting our trust and focus on what really matters—our relationship with the Creator, who determines the fate of our souls.

The fear of the Lord isn't about cowering in dread. It's about living in reverence, fully aware of His holiness and love. It shifts our focus from the here-and-now to the eternal. It reminds us that life is more than the physical; there is an unseen reality that holds greater significance. We don't serve a God who is indifferent to our actions—He cares deeply about our choices, our hearts, and our faithfulness to Him.

Ideally, the fear of God doesn't push us away from him but draws us closer. When we understand the magnitude of who He is, it compels us to live differently. We begin to see sin for what it truly is: separation from the One who holds both life and eternity. And instead of fearing punishment, we fear the idea of being distant from Him. We long to stay close, to live in a way that pleases Him, not out of dread but out of love and awe for who He is.

Reflection Questions:

- How do I approach my relationship with God? Do I hold God in reverence and awe, or do I approach Him too casually, without recognizing His holiness? Consider your attitude when you pray and make decisions—are you seeking to honor Him, or are you taking Him for granted?
- What do my fears reveal about my relationship with God?
- Am I more afraid of what people can do to me, or do I place my trust in God's eternal power and authority?

Reflect on where your fears come from—are they rooted in human concerns or a healthy reverence for God?
- Am I living in a way that reflects a healthy fear of the Lord?
- How does the fear of God impact the way I live? Do my actions show that I value my relationship with Him above all else? Think about whether your life choices align with the reverence you claim to have for God.

THE "JESUS IS MY HOMEBOY" STORY

I remember when they made these "Jesus Is My Homeboy" shirts with a cartoon-like picture of Jesus. These shirts were popular for a minute. People were divided if they were sacrilegious. Some were singing "I Am a Friend of God" by Israel Houghton, quoting the Scriptures about how Jesus calls us His friends (John 15:15), and the same people were upset, feeling the shirts disrespected Jesus. On the surface, it seemed both sides expressed the same idea, but it was a matter of the heart. For some, the song represented a genuine relationship and friendship with Jesus. However, for those same people, the shirts seemed to reduce the reverence of God, creating their own casual version of who they thought He was, similar to what Paul warned about in Romans 1:21-23 when people began to develop their own images of God.

The real issue wasn't the song or the shirt. Neither truly captures the depth of what it means to be close to God—words alone can't do it justice. The meaning behind these things isn't found in the lyrics or the image but in the heart of the person making the statement. The shirts did not bother me. I would personally not wear them because I am concerned about being careful with any image of God. My greater concern is to the person wanting to express their faith. Do you understand whom you pray to and whom you represent? Do you realize that the God of the universe—the Creator of all things, the Holy One—cares deeply for you? That's not something we should take lightly. We should approach God with boldness and reverence, fully aware of who He is in all His glory.

This is why the Bible repeatedly tells us to "fear the Lord." But often, we confuse this biblical reference to fear with the human emotion of fear that would lead us away from God. Human fear, built into our survival instincts, helps protect us from physical danger. That fear keeps us from harm, warning us of risks. There is also a *spirit of fear* that doesn't come from God but from the enemy. This spirit distorts our view of God, distances us from Him, and keeps us from becoming the men He intended us to be.

Second Timothy 1:7 reminds us, "For God has not given us a spirit of fear, but of power, love, and self-discipline." This verse emphasizes that God intends us to live with courage rooted in His love and truth. God's spirit gives us confidence, wisdom, and peace—not the crippling fear that paralyzes and prevents us from walking in our calling.

Similarly, 1 John 4:18 (ESV) says, "There is no fear in love, but perfect love casts out fear. For fear has to do with punishment, and whoever fears has not been perfected in love." When you read this, you understand he is talking about the work of salvation and that assurance we have when we are in right standing with God. The perfect love of Christ expels all fear of judgment.

A spirit of fear keeps us away from God and distorts our understanding of who He is. It makes us think God is harsh or waiting to punish us. But the reality is that God's perfect love drives out all fear. Instead of fearing punishment, we learn to stand in awe of His love, which draws us closer to Him.

This unhealthy fear—one that keeps us away from God, stunts our growth and stops us from maturing—is not the fear of the Lord that Scripture calls us to. The Bible says in Proverbs 1:7 (ESV), "The fear of the Lord is the beginning of knowledge." In Proverbs 9:10, it's called "the beginning of wisdom." This fear, this reverence for God, helps us understand who He is and propels us forward in our relationship with Him. It's not a fear of punishment but a fear of separation—a deep desire to stay close to Him because of who He is.

The fear of the Lord is not about being scared of God's wrath but about recognizing His greatness and realizing that life apart from Him is empty and incomplete.

Psalm 111:10 (ESV) echoes this, saying, "The fear of the Lord is the beginning of wisdom; all those who practice it have a good understanding. His praise endures forever." This verse ties reverence for God to understanding and a life that aligns with His ways. Reverent fear is the fear we should embrace—the kind that draws us closer to Him.

Think of a child who's afraid of the dark. Turning on the light brings temporary comfort, but true peace comes from the presence of a parent nearby. In the same way, I don't want to be separated from God—not because I'm afraid of what He'll do to me but because I know who He is and want to stay close to Him. The fear of the Lord is not about being scared of God's wrath but about recognizing His greatness and realizing that life apart from Him is empty and incomplete.

This is the kind of fear we're talking about—a holy awe that draws us near, protects us, and leads us to the One who can truly keep us safe. Psalm 34:9 (NIV) says, "Fear the LORD, you His holy people, for those who fear him lack nothing." When we live in reverence for God, we walk in His provision, guidance, and grace.

OVERCOMING FEAR

Fear tries to manifest in all areas of a man's life. One of the responsibilities of men is to conquer and overcome fear. Yet, when it comes to the fear of the Lord, we are called not to avoid it but to embrace it—allowing it to keep us close to God. I know this sounds complex, but I believe it's essential for men to become more accustomed to processing these deeper feelings. We need to learn how to apply these concepts to how we interact with the world around us.

Growing up, showing or having fear was considered a sign of weakness. I was afraid to admit I was scared, so I pretended to be someone I wasn't. But that's no way to live. I don't want to live in the bondage of fear, and I don't want you to either. The only One we should fear is God. We shouldn't live in fear of need because our greatest need is Him. We should be afraid of being far from Him—of misrepresenting Him in how we live.

As we continue deeper into this book, we'll discuss the character of a man of God. But it all starts here, with the fear of the Lord. It's what grounds us, realigns us, and keeps us walking the path He has laid for us.

Before we close this chapter, let's take some measurements. Where are you on the target? Do you hit this ring consistently?

Work on this measurement by doing this reverence test.

Answer the following questions and work through the exercise.

MEASUREMENT CHECK
WHERE DO I FALL ON THE REVERENCE TARGET?

This isn't about grading yourself or achieving perfection but about honest self-reflection. For each question, assign yourself one of the following:

Fully Aligned: I feel confident that I am living with reverence and respect for God in this area.

Needs Attention: I know there's room for improvement, and I can identify specific actions to take.

Not Aligned: I struggle in this area and must refocus on building a deeper relationship with God.

1) Attitude Toward God

Question: *When I approach God in prayer, worship, or in my daily life, do I feel a sense of awe and reverence for who He is?*

- Measurement: Reflect on how you approach God. Do you rush into prayer or worship without considering His greatness, or do you take a moment to acknowledge His holiness? Is your relationship with Him casual, or do honor and respect mark it?

- Self-Check: If you feel that you're becoming too casual in your approach to God, try incorporating moments of silence or reflection before you begin prayer or worship. Acknowledge who He is before you proceed with your requests or praises.

2) Fear of Punishment vs. Fear of Separation

Question: *Do I make decisions out of fear of God's punishment, or am I more concerned with being distant from Him?*

- Measurement: Examine your motivations when making life decisions. Are you obeying God out of fear that He will punish you if you don't, or are you driven by a desire to stay close to Him and avoid the separation that comes from sin?
- Self-Check: If your fear is primarily driven by punishment, focus on developing a deeper understanding of God's love. Meditate on verses like 1 John 4:18, which reminds us that "perfect love drives out fear," and cultivate a relationship with Him based on love rather than dread.

3) Daily Life and Reverence

Question: *Does the way I live my life reflect a healthy fear of the Lord?*

- Measurement: Look at your daily choices, actions, and behaviors. Are they marked by integrity, respect for others, and a desire to honor God? Or are you living in a way that disregards His presence in your life?
- Self-Check: If your life choices don't reflect a reverence for God, begin by setting small, intentional actions that honor Him in your everyday life. This could mean serving others more intentionally, being honest even when it's difficult, or

spending more time in God's Word to align your decisions with His will.

NEXT STEPS:

- If you scored "Fully Aligned": Continue nurturing that reverence, but don't become complacent. Seek ways to go even deeper in your relationship with God.
- If you scored "Needs Attention": Identify specific areas in your life that need adjustment and start making minor changes to bring yourself back into alignment with God's will.
- If you scored "Not Aligned": Take time to reflect and pray for God's guidance. Seek wisdom through Scripture and counsel to help restore your reverence for the Lord.

CHAPTER 6

KNOW THE WORD

As we move deeper into our journey of becoming a marksman, we approach the next ring of the target: knowing the Word. If the fear of the Lord is the foundation upon which wisdom is built, then knowing the Word of God is the essential next step in hitting the mark. To grow as men of God, we need to know His Word. The Bible is our guidebook for life, teaching us how to live, how to lead, and how to love. By studying Scripture regularly, we gain the wisdom and strength we need to face life's challenges and lead our families and communities well.

> *"Your word is a lamp to guide my feet and a light for my path."—Psalm 119:105*

The Word of God is one of twelve core values at our church. We state that we want to know the Word intimately and accurately. That core value is important because we want everyone to have a personal connection with the God we see in the Bible. We want to know Him accurately and rightly handle the Word of truth so we will not be led astray. This value of intimacy and accuracy is important for men because they are called to be spiritual leaders in their homes and communities. You must know the Word.

I understand that this can feel overwhelming at first. When I first got saved, I was an uneducated high school dropout; once I learned how to dig deep into the Scriptures, everything changed. The life lessons and character-building it provided shaped my life and molded me into the man I am today. I learned how to be a father even though I did not have a positive example of one. I learned how to conduct business the right way and work unto the Lord. I eventually learned how to be a father, a husband, and a good son through the contents of its writings. I know I did not achieve this on my own. God helped me every step of the way.

That's the beauty of our relationship with God. In that close relationship, we don't have to navigate His Word alone because we have the Holy Spirit, our teacher and guide. As John 14:26 reminds us: "But when the Father sends the Advocate as my representative—that is, the Holy Spirit—He will teach you everything and will remind you of everything I have told you." The Holy Spirit is the key to understanding Scripture. He illuminates the Word and helps us apply it to our lives so that we know what to do in times of trouble and everyday interactions. The Spirit of God works in partnership with the written Word. Together, they reveal deeper truths and help us live according to God's design. This guidance ensures that our walk with God isn't just based on head knowledge or rules we learn but on a living, breathing relationship. That relationship is where the Spirit leads and confirms His truth within us. I learned this lesson on day one—literally.

MY FIRST ENCOUNTER WITH THE WORD

When I first came to Christ, I had a radical, undeniable encounter with God. I walked into a church expecting the quiet Catholic service I was used to. What I found instead was completely different—a full band playing country-style music, clapping, and tambourines—I thought I'd stepped into a cult or some strange movie! I didn't hear a word of the sermon, but during the altar call, I stood in my place and prayed, *God, if you're real, I'll find you here.* I felt God's presence fill me at that moment, and I heard His voice. It was an entire conversation in my mind—I knew God was speaking to me. That conversation changed the direction of my life forever. Later that night, I wanted to experience that feeling again. However, instead of hearing His voice, I was compelled to find a Bible. I didn't know where to start, so I opened it randomly, and it landed on Proverbs 1:10-11 (NKJV).

As I began to read, the words hit me like they were written specifically for my life:

My son, if sinners entice you,
Do not consent.
If they say, "Come with us,
Let us lie in wait to *shed* blood;
Let us lurk secretly for the innocent without cause...."

That verse was a gangster verse. It spoke like He knew I was a certain-minded person. God was speaking to me about my very situation. I was hanging out with the wrong crowd, people who were literally encouraging me to commit violent acts, do crime, and do street life stuff. As I continued reading, it was as if God were sitting next to me, speaking directly into my heart:

Turn at my rebuke;
Surely I will pour out my spirit on you;
I will make my words known to you.—Proverbs 1:23 (NKJV)

That verse became a foundation for my life. God's Spirit would make His Word known to me, and from that night on, I saw the Scriptures as a direct conversation with God. I stayed up all night reading the Bible. His words came alive in a way I'd never experienced before with any other reading. It wasn't just knowledge—it was life-changing truth.

The Word, in partnership with the Holy Spirit, changed me from the inside out. Knowing the Word isn't just about memorizing verses or being able to quote Scripture—it's about allowing the Holy Spirit to speak through the Word to guide, teach, and transform us. It's about the Word being embedded in our hearts. To this day, I don't always hear God's voice audibly—there have only been a few times in my life when that has happened—but He often speaks internally to me, and without fail, He daily speaks directly into my life situations through the written Word. We come to know Him through the living Word of God, found in the Scriptures.

Even as I've studied the Word for over twenty-five years now, taken classes, and sought deeper understanding, I discover more treasure and insight every time through His Word without fail, illuminated by the Holy Spirit.

WHY KNOWING THE WORD MATTERS

Every encounter with God may not feel like an earth-shattering experience. Still, we must remain diligent and disciplined in our approach. It's crucial to understand that knowing the Word isn't just about intellectual knowledge—it's about applying it to our lives.

James 1:22 (author paraphrase) reminds us: "But don't just listen to God's Word. It would help if you did what it says. Otherwise, you are only fooling yourselves."

This verse emphasizes the difference between merely hearing the Word and truly living it out. You see, just as a marksman can't hit the target without practice, we can't live out our faith without practicing what it says. We should immerse ourselves in the Scriptures and learn how to get closer to our goal of being more like Jesus. Knowing the Word helps us:

- **Defend Against Spiritual Attacks**—Like Jesus in the wilderness, we need the Word to stand firm against the enemy. Ephesians 6:17 says, "Put on salvation as your helmet, and take the sword of the Spirit, which is the word of God." I can't stress enough how important this is because we have a real enemy who viciously tries to twist the Word of God to lead us into sin. He did it in the Garden of Eden and continues to do it now. We must know the Word and how to apply it when making the right decisions.
- **Gain Wisdom and Direction**—The Word of God lights our path and guides us in decisions. Psalm 119:105 says, "Your word is a lamp to guide my feet and a light for my path." The Word of God has been my guide as a father, a pastor, and a businessman. I didn't have a formal education, but the principles I found in the Bible have helped me make wise decisions in every area of my life.
- **Grow in Faith**—Romans 10:17 says, "So faith comes from hearing, that is, hearing the Good News about Christ." Knowing the Word strengthens our faith and deepens our trust in God. Learning to handle and interpret Scripture

correctly accelerated my spiritual and personal growth. My life completely changed when I started taking the Word seriously and putting in the work. Many people I knew who didn't approach the study of God's Word with the same dedication never experienced the same growth, success, and change.

- **Know Who We Are**—The Word reveals our true identity in Christ. It helps us align our lives with His purposes. Second Timothy 3:16-17 says: "All Scripture is inspired by God and is useful to teach us what is true and to make us realize what is wrong in our lives. It corrects us when we are wrong and teaches us to do what is right. God uses it to prepare and equip his people to do every good work." We'll discuss this further later in the book, but you will never fully know who you really are without the truth contained in the Bible.

HOW TO KNOW THE WORD

Many men struggle to study the Bible consistently or feel overwhelmed by its depth and length. However, knowing the Word is more than memorizing every verse or reciting it flawlessly; it's about engaging with it regularly and letting it shape your thoughts, actions, and decisions. Here's a simple guide to help you grow in knowing the Word:

1] **Start With a Plan**—Reading the Bible aimlessly can feel overwhelming. A reading plan can guide you through different themes, books, and teachings. Whether reading through the New Testament, focusing on Proverbs, or working through a devotional, having structure helps. One of my favorite quotes from Mike Tyson is, "Everyone has a plan until they get punched in the mouth." That's how I felt when I first tried reading the Bible cover to cover at nineteen. It hit me dead in the mouth, and I didn't finish. Choosing a plan that fits where you are in your walk is essential. If you're new, start with the Gospels or explore the New Testament. Once you've got a foundation, dive into Proverbs or the Old Testament. There are great Bible plans out there—from books to apps. Don't overwhelm yourself or try to reinvent the wheel. Ask your leaders for advice and challenge yourself, but don't get discouraged if you need to pace yourself.

2) **Don't Just Read . . . Study—**There's a difference between reading and studying the Word. When you read, take time to meditate on what you're learning. Ask questions like:
- What is God revealing about Himself?
- How does this apply to my life today?
- How does this passage challenge or encourage me?
- Going deeper into the Word requires deliberate, thought-out action. Reading daily devotions is good, but set aside time to study what you're reading. Get a study Bible or explore tools to help you dig deeper. An excellent place to start is studying the historical context of one of the epistles or focusing on a specific topic.

3) **Memorize Key Scriptures—**Just as a marksman keeps his eye trained on the target, we must keep the Word of God close to our hearts. Memorizing Scripture equips you to recall God's truth in times of need. Start with verses that resonate with you and build on that. Psalm 119:11 says, "I have hidden your word in my heart, that I might not sin against you." There's something powerful about taking Scripture

to heart. Identify key verses that resonate with you on a personal level. Memorize or meditate on them, as the Bible encourages us to "meditate on His Word."

4) Pray the Word—The Bible is God's living Word, and praying it back to Him aligns your heart with His will. As you read, turn what you learn into prayer. For example, if you're reading about trusting God, pray for the strength to trust Him more in your life. The Holy Spirit plays a key role in understanding the Word, so pray before and after your reading. Ask for help applying it to your life. One method I recommend is journaling your thoughts after a reading session. I have pages from my personal devotion times where I've prayed and written down what God revealed to me through the Scriptures.

5) Live It Out—James 1:22-24 says, "But don't just listen to God's Word. You must do what it says. Otherwise, you are only fooling yourselves. For if you listen to the Word and don't obey, it is like glancing at your face in a mirror. You see yourself, walk away, and forget what you look like." The Word isn't just something to read; it's something to live. When the Word shapes our actions, thoughts, and decisions, we begin to align more fully with who God has called us to be. Put into practice one or two things you've learned each time. I've found that the Word becomes alive when you live it out. People who only recite Scripture without putting it into practice often don't grow. They may look the part, but the fruit won't be visible in their family, career, or ministry.

UNDERSTANDING GOD THROUGH THE WORD

Understanding God through His Word is a challenge that every man of God should accept. It needs to be a personal journey, taken seriously and grounded in accountability, with the guidance of the Holy Spirit. One of the best steps you can take is to connect with your pastor or spiritual leaders. Talk to them about your desire to grow in understanding the Word. Scripture tells us in Ephesians 4:11-12:

> *Now these are the gifts Christ gave to the church: the apostles, the prophets, the evangelists, and the pastors and teachers. Their responsibility is to equip God's people to do his work and build up the church, the body of Christ.*

God gave us these leaders to help us grow and equip us for ministry. Asking questions is not only okay but also a sign of moving from simply being a believer to becoming a disciple. Disciples ask questions, seek deeper understanding, and embrace growth.

I want to encourage you to dive deep into personal study. There's a problem I see today, especially with the rise of social media and YouTube—content is often pre-digested for us, much like a bird feeding its young. We've become skilled at repeating what we've heard, but we often struggle to truly digest the Word for ourselves. Even though we have more resources, teaching, and access to sermons than ever before, we're seeing a decline in biblical literacy in the church.

I say this as someone who's still relatively young—I'm only forty-four—but when I got saved, we didn't have the resources we have today. I remember watching preachers on TV, and when the message would just suddenly cut off, they'd ask for $29.99 to hear the rest. I didn't have that kind of money, so I had no choice but to open the Bible and read the verses myself. That ended up being the best thing that could have happened to me.

It's great to have teachers—we need them. They are gifts from God, and we shouldn't take that lightly. But we should also remember the balance in 1 John 2:27, which says:

> *But you have received the Holy Spirit, and he lives within you, so you don't need anyone to teach you what is true. For the Spirit teaches you everything you need to know, and what he teaches is true—it is not a lie. So just as he has taught you, remain in fellowship with Christ.*

This verse doesn't mean that we should disregard teachers or spiritual leaders, but it reminds us that the Holy Spirit is our ultimate guide in understanding and applying the Word of God. He is the One who brings it to life. What John is teaching here is that we should not depend solely on human teaching—especially when it comes to false or misleading teachers—but instead trust the Holy Spirit to reveal the truth to us.

When you approach the Bible with the Holy Spirit as your guide, Scripture becomes more than words on a page—it becomes God's living voice speaking into your life.

It's easy to get caught up in simply following others or relying on someone else's interpretation of Scripture. Still, the Holy Spirit is given to all believers to help us understand God's truth firsthand. This doesn't negate the role of pastors or teachers. We need them in our lives, but it emphasizes the importance of personal engagement with the Word. We should first go to the Holy Spirit for guidance, allowing Him to shape our understanding while also valuing the leaders God has placed in our lives to equip us.

When you approach the Bible with the Holy Spirit as your guide, Scripture becomes more than words on a page—it becomes God's living voice speaking into your life. Real transformation happens in this partnership between the Word and the Holy Spirit.

ACCURACY MATTERS

As we wrap up this chapter, I hope you're feeling inspired to approach the Bible with more purpose and intention. One of the biggest things that changed my life was learning how to read the Bible accurately. Think of it like this: a marksman doesn't just shoot and hope to hit the right target—he takes careful aim. In the same way, as men and leaders, we need to do our best to understand Scripture clearly and accurately.

Here are three simple principles to help:

1) **Let Scripture Explain Scripture**—The Bible often interprets itself. When trying to understand a verse, compare it with other verses. The Bible is one complete story, and different parts help explain each other.
2) **Look at the Context**—It's essential to know the background, the people, and the culture behind a passage.

Understanding who it was written for helps us apply it correctly to our lives today.

3) **Don't Force Your Own Meaning**—Instead of trying to make the Bible say what you want, look for what it's actually saying. Let God's Word speak for itself.

> You don't have to be a scholar; just be open to learning and growing. God will do the rest.

Wherever you are on your journey, remember this: the Bible's central theme is to reveal Jesus. From Genesis to Revelation, it shows us who He is and how we can live like Him. So, as you dive deeper, keep your focus on seeing Jesus in the Word. You don't have to be a scholar; just be open to learning and growing. God will do the rest.

MEASUREMENT CHECK
DOES MY LIFE ALIGN WITH GOD'S WORD?

This isn't about perfection but about reflecting on your journey with the Word of God. For each question, evaluate yourself using one of the following categories:

Fully Aligned: I feel confident in my engagement with God's Word and how I apply it to my life.

Needs Attention: I know there's room for improvement and can identify specific actions to take.

Not Aligned: I struggle in this area and need to refocus on building a deeper relationship with Scripture.

1) Consistency in Reading

Question: *Do I regularly read and engage with the Bible?*
- Measurement: Reflect on how often you read the Word. Are you consistent with a reading plan, or do you go long periods without opening your Bible?
- Self-Check: If you struggle with consistency, start with a small goal—whether it's reading a chapter a day or following a devotional. Remember, it's about quality, not just quantity.

2) Studying vs. Surface Reading

Question: *When I read the Bible, do I take the time to study and meditate on it, or do I skim through it?*
- Measurement: Evaluate whether you're diving deep into the Word. Do you understand the context of what you're reading and apply it to your life, or do you just get through the reading without much thought?
- Self-Check: If you're only skimming, try adding study tools like a study Bible, commentary, or even journaling what you're learning.

3) Applying the Word

Question: *Do I apply what I learn from Scripture to my daily decisions and actions?*
- Measurement: Think about your behavior at home, at work, and in your relationships. Do you let the Word shape your actions and guide your choices, or is there a disconnect between reading Scripture and living it out?
- Self-Check: Start by making a small change—apply one lesson from your daily Bible reading to your interactions with family or colleagues.

4) Memorizing Scripture

Question: *Am I storing God's Word in my heart so that I can recall it in times of need?*

- Measurement: Assess whether you are actively working to memorize critical scriptures that will help you in times of trial or temptation.
- Self-Check: If this is an area that needs work, begin with one or two key verses that speak to your current struggles or areas of growth.

5) Using the Word as a Weapon

Question: *Do I know how to use Scripture to defend against spiritual attacks, like Jesus did in the wilderness?*

- Measurement: Reflect on whether you know how to use specific verses to combat fear, temptation, or doubt. Are you confident in turning to Scripture when you're under attack?
- Self-Check: If you struggle here, start by identifying areas of your life where the enemy attacks and find relevant scriptures to arm yourself with.

NEXT STEPS

- **If you scored "Fully Aligned":** Continue to grow in your engagement with Scripture, but don't become complacent. Ask God to reveal deeper truths and ways to apply the Word to new areas of your life.
- **If you scored "Needs Attention":** Identify where you can improve and take specific steps. Start small—whether it's a reading plan or setting aside time for study and meditation.
- **If you scored "Not Aligned":** Don't get discouraged. Take it as an opportunity to reset. Pray for God to give you a fresh

hunger for His Word and seek accountability to help you stay on track.

CHAPTER 7
MATURE AS MEN

In darts, the inner rings of a target are worth more points because they are harder to hit and closer to the bullseye. Hitting these next rings will challenge you on a deeper level. Maturity isn't just about age—it's about developing and displaying the character that aligns with God's Word and purpose for our lives. Maturity doesn't happen overnight. It's the process of growing in our faith. Maturing means learning from our good or bad experiences and allowing them to shape our character. As we mature, we develop qualities like patience, self-control, and perseverance, and we become more like Christ in how we live and treat others.

Paul puts it plainly in 1 Corinthians 13:11: "When I was a child, I spoke and thought and reasoned as a child. But when I grew up, I put away childish things."

Love is at the core of maturity because it transforms our actions and our relationships with others.

If you look deeper into the context of this passage, Paul is writing about the importance of love and how it matters in everything we do. He describes what love should look like and how it can define our character.

That verse perfectly captures what it means to mature: understanding love in depth and complexity. Maturing means putting away childish speech, thoughts, and actions and embracing who we are in God's love. This love then becomes the foundation of what we do, what we say, and how we live.

A mature man doesn't just do things for the sake of doing them—he does them with love and care. I can't imagine a better way to describe maturity than understanding love. Love is at the core of maturity because it transforms our actions and our relationships with others.

Men, if we can approach our daily lives with mature love—the kind of love that God describes in 1 Corinthians 13—not only will we feel more fulfilled, but we will also make a more significant impact in the things we do and the people we interact with. The love of God enabled Paul to endure tremendous hardship, and it will allow us to, also. The Bible teaches that "for the joy set before him [Jesus] endured the cross" (Hebrews 12:2, NIV). What joy could there be in suffering if not for love and relationships?

Mature men understand that there's more to our actions than surface-level emotions. Before Christ, my childish behavior cost me jobs and opportunities early in life. My unwillingness to confront my immature nature hurt the people I loved and got in the way of growing up. I was a hammer. Everything was a nail. Just about everything came out in anger until I confronted the hurt, broken child I was.

A CHILDHOOD LESSON

Growing up, I was really into comics, fantasy books, and superhero shows. One of my favorite shows was *Voltron*. I still have the Voltron toy in my collection to this day. I hope Paul did not mean to put childish things away like toys because I still have many of them.

What made Voltron so cool was that five separate robot lions came together to form one unstoppable robot—Voltron, the defender of the universe.[2]

I hold onto those good memories because, honestly, my childhood was filled with a lot of bad experiences, pain, and trauma that I carried into adulthood. Like many men, I was exposed to things too young, things that distorted my view of how to process emotions and be a man. The truth is that childhood never entirely leaves us. That's why shows like *Transformers*[3] and *Ninja Turtles*[4] hold such lasting power—nostalgia is powerful. We carry habits and attitudes from childhood, both good and bad, into adulthood.

Those shows were an escape from the reality of pain I was living in. I picked up a lot of bad character traits from the trauma and issues of my life, traits that affected me even as an adult.

---

2 *Voltron*, Joaquim Dos Santos and Eugene Lee (September 10, 1984; St. Louis, MO: World Events Productions), Television.
3 *The Transformers*, Matt Youngberg (September 17, 1984; New York, NY: Sunbow Productions), Television.
4 *Teenage Mutant Ninja Turtles*, Fred Wolf (December 28, 1987; Burbank, CA: Fred Wolf Films), Television.

But like many men, I learned to bury those feelings and press on—just "man up."

There's a stigma in our culture that tells men they shouldn't deal with emotional issues, but burying them only leads to problems later. A study in *Medical News Today* showed that cultural stigma around mental health in men has contributed to higher rates of depression, suicide, and anger issues. Men are also four times more likely than women to die by suicide.[5] If we leave these issues unresolved, they resurface at the worst times, affecting our marriages, families, careers, and daily lives. Just like Voltron needed to come together as one to defeat their enemies, there are five key abilities that we, as men, need to form in our lives to overcome these challenges. And, like Voltron, we can only develop these abilities with God's help.

In Acts 1:8, Jesus tells His disciples: "But you will receive power when the Holy Spirit comes upon you. And you will be my witnesses, telling people about me everywhere—in Jerusalem, throughout Judea, in Samaria, and to the ends of the earth."

The word "power" is *dunamis* in Greek, which means "ability." The Holy Spirit gives us the ability to do what seems impossible. And with His power, we can develop these five abilities in our lives:

1) Responsibility

Taking responsibility for yourself and others is the first mark of a mature man. It's a scary thought because responsibility comes with weight, but being a man of God requires responsibility. I used to blame everyone else for my problems: my dad, my teachers, my

---

[5] Center for Disease Control and Prevention, *Suicide Data and Statistics* (CDC Suicide Prevention, 2024).

friends, and even God. But maturity came when I realized I had to take responsibility for my life. No more blaming others—only then could I grow and change.

2) Accountability

We are accountable to God and each other. We must raise our standards as men of God. We don't get to escape accountability and shouldn't want to. Accountability holds us to God's standard.

The enemy works hard to keep us isolated and prevents us from opening up to anyone. But God already knows your heart, your struggles, and your sins. He accepts you anyway. Surround yourself with brothers you trust and hold each other accountable.

Accountability comes from trust, and trust comes from knowing the Word. Many men don't know God's Word and operate based on feelings rather than truth. We need to hold ourselves accountable to the Word of God.

3) Availability

The best ability is availability. It doesn't matter how skilled you are if you're not there when you're needed. You can be as talented as LeBron James, but if you're not in the game, you're not helping the team.

We must be available to our families, emotionally and physically. So many of us were hurt by absent fathers. Men, we need to change that story for the next generation.

God is looking for men who will say, "Here I am. Send me" (Isaiah 6:8).

4) Vulnerability

This is the hardest one for most men. Vulnerability can open us up to attack or harm—emotionally and physically. Vulnerability is not a sign of weakness; it's a sign of strength.

It's hard to hear the truth, hard to admit our failures, and hard to ask for help. But growth happens when we're vulnerable before God and others. When we allow God to work on the hidden issues of our hearts, He brings healing.

5) Power (Dunamis)

The Holy Spirit empowers all these abilities. Without Him, we can't consistently practice them. As Acts 1:8 says, the Holy Spirit gives us the ability to be witnesses and live as men of God.

THE LESSON

Every episode of *Voltron* ends the same way. Each lion fights the enemy on its own, but they get defeated individually. It's only when they come together as one that they can overcome.[6] The lesson for us is the same. We can't do this on our own. We need brothers to stand with us and God's help to be the men He's called us to be. Some men will be strong, and some will be weak. We can disciple, encourage, and impart until we become the better version of ourselves.

When we unite with responsibility, accountability, availability, vulnerability, and the power of God's Holy Spirit, we become unstoppable, like Voltron.

PERSONAL STORY: A TIME TO GROW UP

As a young and eager nineteen-year-old starting my journey in electronics, I was self-educating, reading daily, and doing everything I could to become a better version of myself, trying to become the man God called me to be. I grew up with a street mentality even though I was not of the roughest of streets. I grew

---

6 *Voltron*, Joaquim Dos Santos and Eugene Lee, Television.

up in Sunnyvale but got into plenty of trouble. I grew up without much money, and when I looked for a better job, I bought slacks and ties from Goodwill. It was embarrassing, and the clothes were ugly, but I needed to change. I would practice in front of a mirror to talk and walk more professionally. I had to work hard to change how I spoke, as I used a lot of slang. I even read the dictionary to learn new words to sound more professional.

> **Sometimes, we have to block out the outside noise and follow the path God sets before us.**

This job opportunity happened during the dot-com boom in Silicon Valley, and through God's blessing, I had the chance to break into the multi-billion-dollar electronics industry. I started as a temp answering phones, but it quickly became an opportunity to change my future. I was given the chance to get hired full-time and choose between sales or engineering, but I had to grow up fast. Some of my friends laughed, calling me a sellout because I was drastically changing. But I knew this was my opportunity to leave behind my rough upbringing. While they had their parents to fall back on, they didn't understand my situation. I was living in a trailer with a hose for a shower behind a house full of several families on the East Side of San Jose. I had no other option but to make it work.

Sometimes, we have to block out the outside noise and follow the path God sets before us. The process of "selling out"—wearing Goodwill clothes and learning to walk and talk differently—was part of God's work to humble me and deal with my pride. God can work with a humble heart. But the man who won't humble himself before God and refuses to do what He asks shouldn't expect God's favor when he faces situations of dire need.

By trusting in God and applying His principles, I became the top salesman in the company within two years and bought a house at twenty-one in one of the most expensive markets in the US. This didn't happen because I stayed the same—it happened because I allowed myself to grow into the man God wanted me to be. I realized that in every area of life—family, career, and ministry—God was giving me the opportunity to glorify Him.

MATURITY AS A SPIRITUAL LEADER

Maturity means knowing what God is leading you to do and applying His Word to your situation. We must mature spiritually so that we are not swayed by every new idea or false teaching that comes our way.

Ephesians 4:14-15 says:

> *Then we will no longer be immature like children. We won't be tossed and blown about by every wind of new teaching. We will not be influenced when people try to trick us with lies so clever they sound like the truth. Instead, we will speak the truth in love, growing in every way more and more like Christ, who is the head of his body, the church.*

Spiritual maturity gives us the discernment to know when something isn't aligned with God's truth. It helps us lead with integrity, stay grounded in His Word, and live with purpose.

WHAT MATURITY LOOKS LIKE

Men need to understand what true maturity looks like. Once again, it's more than just getting older—it's about developing spiritual, emotional, and relational maturity.

Spiritual Maturity

Spiritual maturity is a deep commitment to walking closely with God, being rooted in prayer, studying His Word, and being devoted to serving others. Many men have a surface-level spirituality, and that often happens because they've learned the spiritual language but have yet to process its meaning. The key to maturing in all areas of life is to ask yourself, *How deep are my roots?* Your spiritual life in public should be an overflow of an even deeper private devotion. A mature man's private time with God will speak louder than any public ministry or action.

Colossians 1:10 says, "Then the way you live will always honor and please the Lord and your lives will produce every kind of good fruit. All the while, you will grow as you learn to know God better and better."

This verse emphasizes that spiritual maturity is a journey where we continue to grow as we get to know God better. It's not about arriving at a destination but about continually walking with God and letting Him shape our hearts. Spiritual maturity produces real, lasting fruit in our lives, which will show up in how we live, how we love, and how we serve.

Emotional Maturity

Emotional maturity is tested in how we respond to challenges. Instead of reacting out of anger, fear, or aggression, we learn to respond with self-control, patience, and other fruits of the Spirit. It means staying emotionally present under challenging situations rather than running away when things get uncomfortable. I've personally had to overcome destructive habits by digging deep and addressing the root causes of my emotional scars. This process takes time, but it starts by learning to pause, process, and respond—filtering everything through God's help.

James 1:19 gives us the key: "You must all be quick to listen, slow to speak, and slow to get angry."

This verse reminds us that emotional maturity starts with listening—both to God and to others. It's about slowing down enough to hear, reflect, and let God shape our reactions. Too many men are quick to speak or act out of emotion, but true maturity is found in learning to control those impulses and respond with wisdom.

Relational Maturity

Relational maturity is about treating others with love, respect, and patience. It's easy to fall into the trap of fault-finding, especially when disagreements arise, but that's not the way we are called to live. I used to swing from one extreme to the next, thinking everything was all or nothing. That's no way to handle relationships. Just because there's a disagreement doesn't mean you're enemies. We need to work through our differences, sharpening one another as the Scriptures say.

Ephesians 4:2 teaches: "Always be humble and gentle. Be patient with each other, making allowance for each other's faults because of your love."

This verse encourages us to practice humility and gentleness, especially when it's challenging. Maturity in relationships involves recognizing that no one is perfect and allowing space for each other's imperfections. Marriage requires this approach to work genuinely. This mindset is what makes a relationship unique and special, providing room for individuals to be themselves and to navigate through their faults and insecurities together. We're called to approach every relationship—whether with our spouse, children, or brothers in Christ—with patience and grace, allowing love to guide us rather than pride or selfishness. This will bring the best out of each other.

As Proverbs 27:17 says, "As iron sharpens iron, so a friend sharpens a friend." Our relationships should challenge us to grow, not drive us apart.

BARRIERS TO MATURITY

When you look at your life, growth often comes down to one or two significant changes that need to happen for true transformation. A lot of times, it's those significant stones blocking the path, and once they're removed, the smaller ones start to fall away. Sometimes, what holds us back from maturing is our own pride, laziness, or fear of change. We need to examine ourselves honestly and be willing to let go of old habits and mindsets that hinder us from growing.

Key Verse: "Fools have no interest in understanding; they only want to air their own opinions" (Proverbs 18:2). Most of the time, we already know what these barriers are—it's just hard to actually do something about them. Start the work now, and trust

God in His Word. The One who started the process is faithful to complete it.

PRACTICAL STEPS TO MATURITY
1) Take Responsibility
Own your actions and choices. Stop blaming others and recognize the power you have in your own growth.
Key Verse: "Each of you must take responsibility for doing the creative best you can with your own life" (Galatians 6:5, MSG).
2) Seek Wisdom
Surround yourself with wise counsel and be intentional about your spiritual growth. Wisdom isn't just found—it's pursued.
Key Verse: "Walk with the wise and become wise; associate with fools and get in trouble" (Proverbs 13:20).
3) Practice Self-Discipline
Build habits that develop your character, not destroy it. Discipline is challenging, but it produces lasting fruit.
Key Verse: "No discipline seems pleasant at the time, but painful. Later on, however, it produces a harvest of righteousness and peace for those who have been trained by it" (Hebrews 12:11, NIV).

PRESS ON TOWARD MATURITY
Maturing as a man is a lifelong journey. It's not about arriving at perfection but continuing to grow, becoming more like Christ with each step. Philippians 3:14 says, "I press on to reach the end of the race and receive the heavenly prize for which God, through Christ Jesus, is calling us." Keep pressing forward, trusting that as you mature, you will be better equipped to fulfill your calling and lead others into this same journey of growth.

MEASUREMENT CHECK
AM I MATURING AS A MAN?

This self-assessment isn't about achieving perfection but about honest self-reflection and identifying areas of growth. For each question, give yourself one of the following ratings:

Fully Mature: I feel confident that I am consistently growing in this area.

Needs Attention: I know there's room for improvement, and I can identify steps to take.

Not Mature: I struggle in this area and need to focus on growing here.

1) Attitude Toward Responsibility

Question: Do I take ownership of my actions, decisions, and the roles I play, or do I tend to shift blame onto others?

- Measurement: Reflect on how you respond when things go wrong. Are you quick to take responsibility, or do you find yourself blaming others—your past, circumstances, or people around you?
- Self-Check: If you avoid responsibility, consider taking ownership of both your successes and failures. Recognize that responsibility is a key mark of maturity.

2) Emotional Responses

Question: How do I react to challenges or difficult situations—do I respond with patience and self-control, or do I let anger and frustration take over?

- Measurement: Think about the last time you faced a stressful situation. Did you stay calm and handle it maturely, or did you react impulsively or in anger?

- Self-Check: If you struggle with emotional responses, remember James 1:19: "You must all be quick to listen, slow to speak, and slow to get angry." Work on pausing before reacting and allowing God's Word to shape your responses.

3) Growth in Knowledge of God

Question: Am I intentional about growing in my relationship with God through studying His Word, prayer, and seeking wisdom from others?

- Measurement: Examine your spiritual habits. Are you consistently spending time in God's Word, or are you coasting in your spiritual life?
- Self-Check: If your growth in knowing God has stagnated, commit to a plan that challenges you to go deeper in your walk with God. Surround yourself with wise counsel and seek to be intentional about spiritual maturity.

4) Relational Maturity

Question: Do I treat others—especially my family and friends—with love, patience, and respect, even when disagreements arise?

- Measurement: Reflect on how you handle conflicts. Do you work through differences with grace, or do you let pride, anger, or resentment get in the way?
- Self-Check: If you find yourself often in conflict, focus on Ephesians 4:2: "Always be humble and gentle. Be patient with each other, making allowance for each other's faults because of your love." Relationships should build you and others up, not tear you apart.

5) Availability

Question: Am I present for my family, friends, and responsibilities, or do I avoid situations where I'm needed?

- Measurement: Consider how available you are—emotionally, spiritually, and physically. Are you making time for the people who matter, or are you always too busy or distracted?
- Self-Check: If you struggle with being present, work on being more intentional about your time. Isaiah 6:8 says: "Here I am. Send me." Make yourself available before God and others.

NEXT STEPS:
- If you scored "Fully Mature": You are consistently growing in the areas of responsibility, self-discipline, emotional control, and relationships. Keep pressing on! Continue to strengthen your walk with God and lead others by example.
- If you scored "Needs Attention": You're aware of where you need to grow but struggle with consistency. Identify one or two key areas to work on. Create a plan and take small, consistent steps toward growth.
- If you scored "Not Mature": You find it challenging to embrace responsibility, self-discipline, and accountability. Don't be discouraged—maturity is a lifelong process. Ask God for wisdom and take the first step by addressing one area where you need growth.

CHAPTER 8
KNOW WHO YOU ARE

I remember being kicked out of school, and the vice principal essentially told me I was a lost cause. I was too far behind, and they suggested I drop out and get a warehouse job. Others told me I would end up just like my father and wouldn't amount to anything. For years, I let those words shape who I thought I was instead of letting Christ define me. We're all being influenced daily, whether by people, society, or the role models we look up to and culture. We must know our identity in Christ so that others won't define who we are.

Jesus defines our possibilities, not the world.

Today, I pastor an amazing group of people in San Jose and have been fortunate enough to do many things for God across the country, from designing products to releasing Christian music and clothing that have a global reach to working on technology that's used in the military, medical industries, and even at Universal Studios in Florida. I never thought that any of this was possible growing up. It's similar to Acts 4:13, when the people recognized the disciples as ordinary men but noted that they had been with Jesus. That's the difference—Jesus defines our possibilities, not the world. I love this verse because it shows that the rest of the world will recognize something different about ordinary men who spend time with Jesus. That relationship with Jesus gives me value and purpose. When you are close to Jesus, you are valuable.

The Bible tells us we are created in God's image (Genesis 1:27), and temporary things like our success, reputation, or possessions do not determine our worth. Our value is rooted in Him, the Creator. Only then can our actions reflect whom we truly belong to—God.

As we move through this chapter, open your heart and ask yourself if you see yourself the way God sees you. For some of you, this might be the first time you get an accurate picture of what God wants you to become as a husband, a father, a son, or a brother. James 1:23-24 tells us, "For if you listen to the word and don't obey, it is like glancing at your face in a mirror. You see yourself, walk away, and forget what you look like." Our identity isn't just in what we do or how we appear—it goes much deeper than that.

As you walk through the steps of maturing in faith, the Bible begins to reveal who you are meant to be. Scripture tells us that we are all created in the image of God (Genesis 1:27). Through Christ, we gain the right to become children of God (John 1:12), adopted into His family—not by our blood but by His choice. Becoming His children brings us into a covenant relationship with God, where we are not just His servants but co-heirs with Christ. As Romans 8:16-17 tells us:

"For his Spirit joins with our Spirit to affirm that we are God's children. And since we are his children, we are his heirs. In fact, together with Christ, we are heirs of God's glory. But if we are to share his glory, we must also share his suffering."

Being a child of God gives us purpose, direction, and authority. But this inheritance shouldn't be taken lightly. We are not to act like spoiled children who do whatever we want. Instead, we must carry this responsibility with the highest level of regard and reverence. That's why understanding the fear of God, knowing His Word, and maturing in our faith are crucial before we can honestly understand who we are in Christ. These foundations are necessary to grasp the identity He has given us entirely.

Romans 8:17 tells us that because we are co-heirs with Christ, we share not only in His glory but also in His sufferings. There is a weight to God's glory—a responsibility that comes with the privilege of being called His children. This call and responsibility require maturity and a willingness to endure hardships while walking in the blessings.

Paul's reminder that we share in Christ's suffering highlights the trials of the Christian life. Just as Christ endured suffering before being glorified, we will face challenges. But it is through these trials that we become more like Him, and as we persevere, we are transformed. The identity that we are co-heirs of these promises focuses on the blessings of heaven and living in alignment with God's purpose here on earth, even when it's hard.

In essence, our identity in Christ isn't just about receiving promises or blessings. It's about embracing the whole picture—our purpose, the weight of His glory, and the challenges that come with it. When we understand this is how life goes, we walk in our true identity with reverence and gratitude. We know that every part of our journey, even the suffering, is part of being aligned with Christ and connects us to something bigger that will work out for our good, so we don't get discouraged or give up.

THE STRUGGLE OF IDENTITY

Even with these truths in Scripture, the world constantly tries to distort our identity. It pushes false narratives of what it means to be successful, what it means to be a man, and what it means to live a meaningful life. Often, we struggle with comparison, insecurity, and fear of failure because we forget who we are in Christ. We allow the opinions of others, our mistakes, or the pressures of society to define us. That's a dangerous path to follow.

Knowing who you are in God doesn't mean you'll never struggle with doubt or insecurity. Still, it does mean you have a foundation to return to when those struggles arise.

PERSONAL STORY: THE FIGHT FOR IDENTITY

There was a defining moment in my life. I found myself wrestling with the direction God wanted me to take. I had a successful electronics business, a family needing my attention, and a growing ministry pulling me in multiple directions. At the same time, I was offered my first church to pastor, and my Christian clothing company, which was tied to the ministry, was gaining traction through events and concerts. Doors were opening up, and opportunities were everywhere. I was at a crossroads, unsure whether to focus on being a pastor, growing my business, or fully being present as a family man. The weight of these decisions left me feeling overwhelmed and uncertain about where to go.

Even though I was doing a lot, I had lost touch with who I was.

Needing clarity, I reached out to Dr. Sam Huddleston, a man I deeply respect. During this meeting, he grabbed a whiteboard, and we laid out everything I was juggling—my business, ministry, family, and potential future decisions. As he walked through it all, he said something that has stuck with me all these years. Even though I was doing a lot, I had lost touch with who I was. My identity had become tangled in all the decisions I was making. I was basing my identity on what I was doing and not who I belonged to.

Dr. Huddleston said, "The problem isn't whether you can succeed—you can succeed at anything because that's how God made you." He blessed us with lots of giftings, but that means nothing if we are not close to Jesus. We are nothing if we are not close to Jesus. Jesus even tried to tell us in John 15:5, "Apart from me you can do nothing."

Dr. Huddleston asked me, "Who would you be if you weren't doing all these things? Would you be content with just having a relationship with Jesus?"

Those words struck me deeply. I realized I had been forming my identity around what I was doing, not who I was in Christ. Even though I was achieving a lot in business, ministry, and life, my personal devotion to Jesus had taken a backseat. That conversation changed my perspective. He gave me a book, *The Divine Mentor*[7], and I went home and readjusted my priorities. I made

---

[7] Wayne Cordeiro, *The Divine Mentor: Growing Your Faith as You Sit at the Feet of the Savior* (Ada, MI: Bethany House Publishers, 2008).

a decision then: I am a follower of Christ first. My relationship with Him is what defines me, not my success or accomplishments.

To this day, I've passed on that same advice to other men and handed out that same book numerous times. Too often, we build our identity on what we do rather than who we are. But our true identity comes from our closeness to Jesus. The fight for identity isn't about achieving things that make us more like Christ; it's about being so close to Him that we reflect His light and His character. Most of us, simply put, are products of whom we spend the most time with. We adapt to our environment and become like the people closest to us. Every time I distance myself from Him, I revert back to my old self.

My pastor, Mitch Thurman, always used to say, "You can say what you want, but you impart who you are." True impartation happens through close relationships." The closer you are to Jesus, the more you realize that's who you are meant to be. I am not a follower of Jesus because of all the things I do for Him; I am His because I choose to be close to Him, and He loves me enough to draw close to me. As the Bible says, "Draw near to God and He will draw near to you" (James 4:8, NKJV). Our identity flows out of that intimacy with Christ. When we draw near to Him, we begin to reflect more of who He is.

Our goal is to be more like Him, but sometimes we fall short. I am still working toward a finished product, even as I write this book. I am ambitious and driven, and it's hard for me to slow down. But no matter how busy life gets, I always come back to the same conclusion: maintaining a healthy view of who I am in Christ is what matters most, and I adjust my life accordingly.

Every step leading up to this moment, through every ring, is meant to bring you closer to seeing what and who truly matters in your life. When you put God first, deny yourself, value family, and uphold ministry, you stay on track to get closer and closer to the target.

Men, it would help if you saw who you truly are, your worth, and your value. Christ died so you could be close to Him. He made a way so we no longer live according to our sinful nature but by the Spirit of God. Through that relationship, through the Holy Spirit, we become aware of the truth, and the truth sets us free from slavery and fear. Our identity is affirmed, and the Spirit is given to us as a guarantee of our inheritance:

> *For his Spirit joins with our Spirit to affirm that we are God's children. And since we are his children, we are his heirs. In fact, together with Christ, we are heirs of God's glory. But if we are to share his glory, we must also share his suffering.* —Romans 8:16-17

This is who you truly are. A healthy view of yourself begins with knowing God.

BARRIERS TO KNOWING WHO YOU ARE

The enemy is continually working to distort your identity. Here are a few common barriers to knowing who you are:

1) Comparison

Constantly comparing yourself to others will steal your joy and undermine your sense of self-worth. The Bible warns against this. As discussed in a previous chapter, comparison will kill your calling. Your journey is uniquely yours—no one else can walk it for you. Although we strive to meet God's standards, consistently measuring yourself against others will ultimately hurt you.

Galatians 6:4 says, "Pay careful attention to your own work, for then you will get the satisfaction of a job well done, and you won't need to compare yourself to anyone else."

We each have a unique purpose, and comparison only distracts us from fulfilling it.

2] Past Mistakes

Many men struggle to move beyond their past failures, allowing them to define their present and future. But God's grace is bigger than our mistakes. Conviction that leads to transformation comes from God; condemnation that brings self-destruction and loathing is from the enemy. God is not holding your sins against you—so why are you?

Romans 8:1 reminds us: "So now there is no condemnation for those who belong to Christ Jesus."

When you belong to Christ, your past no longer defines you, and you are free to walk in the new identity He has given you.

3] Worldly Definitions of Success

The world often tells us that our value is based on our bank account, job title, or social status. However, redefining success according to God's Word is crucial for maintaining a healthy self-view.

Mark 8:36 (ESV) asks, "For what does it profit a man to gain the whole world and forfeit his soul?"

True success comes from living out God's purpose, not chasing the world's version of success.

PRACTICAL STEPS TO KNOWING WHO YOU ARE

Here are a few ways to grow in understanding your identity in Christ:

1) Reflect on Scripture

Make it a daily habit to meditate on verses that speak to your identity in Christ. Ask God to reveal deeper truths about who He says you are.

2) Surround Yourself With Truth

Spend time with other believers who will speak truth into your life and remind you of who you are. Community is vital for helping us stay grounded in our identity.

3) Reject the Lies

When lies about your worth and identity come, take them captive and make them obedient to Christ (2 Corinthians 10:5). Replace them with the truth found in God's Word.

KNOW YOURSELF

As difficult as it can be to look inward and examine who you truly are, it's a necessary step in your journey. When you dig past the layers of flaws, mistakes, past hurts, and weaknesses, you'll discover there's nothing there that God didn't already know when He chose you. He saw all those things, and yet He still died for you and desires a relationship with you. This truth gives us freedom—we no longer have to live according to that old sinful nature. As Paul wrote, "Who will deliver me from this body of death? Thanks be to God through Jesus Christ our Lord!" (Romans 7:24-25, ESV) It's not our efforts but Christ's power that transforms us.

➢ God's love defines you, and nothing can change that.

God knows you thoroughly, and He will continue to transform you. But you must keep striving for the principles we've discussed throughout this book—applying them, trusting Him, and allowing Him to shape your identity. It's a journey of continuous growth; along the way, you'll appreciate the process.

It's important to remind yourself of who you are in Christ. I have markers—times of clarity when I knew exactly what God said about me. I hold onto those moments because they guide me through times of uncertainty. No matter how long we've been following Christ, we all need those reminders of who we are in Him. So, when the doubts come, when you feel lost, go back to those markers and remember: God's love defines you, and nothing can change that.

MEASUREMENT CHECK
DO I KNOW WHO I AM IN CHRIST?

This self-assessment helps you evaluate how well you understand your identity in Christ. Rate yourself on each question:

Fully Aligned: I feel confident in this area and am growing.

Needs Attention: I see room for growth and can identify steps to take.

Not Aligned: I struggle here and need to focus on this area.

1) Self-Worth in Christ

Question: Is my value rooted in God's Word, or do I let the opinions of others shape how I see myself?

- Self-Check: If you rely on the world's approval, meditate on verses like Genesis 1:27 to remind yourself you are created in God's image.

2) Freedom From Past Mistakes

Question: Have I accepted God's grace and moved past my failures, or do I let guilt define me?

- Self-Check: Reflect on Romans 8:1. If guilt lingers, give it to God, knowing that in Christ, there is no condemnation.

3) True Success vs. Worldly Success

Question: Do I define success based on God's purpose for me, or am I chasing worldly measures of success (money, status)?

- Self-Check: Consider Mark 8:36—what does it mean to you to gain the world but lose your soul? Focus on living out God's calling.

4) Reliance on God

Question: Do I lean into my relationship with Jesus for my identity, or am I letting my achievements and roles define me?

- Self-Check: Reflect on James 4:8. Commit to drawing near to God to discover more of who you are in Him.

NEXT STEPS:

- If you scored "Fully Aligned": Keep pressing forward! You see yourself as God sees you and are confident that you are a co-heir with Christ.
- If you scored "Needs Attention": Choose one or two areas to focus on and make small, intentional changes in those areas. Focus on Bible verses stating who you are and the work Christ completed on the cross to make you that person.

- If you scored "Not Aligned": Don't be discouraged. Ask God for guidance and begin by addressing one area where you need growth. You don't have to tackle everything at once—just take one step toward realizing you are God's precious child and a co-heir with Christ.

CHAPTER 9
BE LIKE JESUS

The entire focus of this book is aimed at one target: becoming men who are more like Jesus and genuinely follow and live as closely to the example Jesus set in His life and ministry. The reality is that we won't always perfectly reflect Him. Regardless, our goal is to do our best. This becomes especially important in how we love and value our families, conduct ourselves in ministry, and represent the gospel to the world. Jesus called us "the light of the world" (Matthew 5:14), meaning our lives should shine His truth and love into the darkness around us.

We are His body on earth, continuing His work. As Paul tells us in 1 Corinthians 12:27 (NIV): "Now you are the body of Christ, and each one of you is a part of it."

This verse emphasizes that we are not merely imitators of Jesus but participants in His ongoing mission. We are part of His body, and each of us plays a unique role in carrying forward the work He began—in the way we live out our personal relationships, work, or ministry. All our interactions are opportunities for us to glorify God.

To live like Jesus, we must first recognize that becoming like Him is not something we can accomplish through our strength or effort. Ephesians 2:8-9 (NIV) reminds us: "For it is by grace you have been saved, through faith—and this is not from yourselves, it is the gift of God—not by works, so that no one can boast."

Our transformation into salvation directly results from His grace, not our own works. However, we have a part to play in becoming Christ-like through repentance, deliberate effort, and acts of obedience. All glory and power belong to Him, and only through him can we be transformed.

> **The more closely we walk with Him, the more we become His representatives to a world that desperately needs His light.**

Most men struggle with this transformation due to one of two issues: a lack of faith or obedience. Either we don't believe it's possible, or we are unwilling to obey what He has called us to do to make it possible. To be like Jesus, we need both faith and obedience.

The change starts from within, as we connect with Jesus's heart—His motives, mindset, work ethic, and love for people. It's about allowing the Holy Spirit to mold us into the people God has called us to be.

Being like Jesus is not just about copying His outward actions but being transformed inwardly to reflect His heart in everything we do. The more closely we walk with Him, the more we become His representatives to a world that desperately needs His light.

WHAT IT MEANS TO BE LIKE JESUS

I once heard a preacher say, "You might be the only Jesus some people will ever see." That truth has stuck with me, especially when I think about my dad. As strained as our relationship was, I realized I might have been the clearest example of Christ he had ever witnessed in his life. Your witness matters, especially for the people in your circle. Our church reaches many people who think they don't belong in church, and some may never step foot in a church. Unless they are reached outside the church, what hope would they have? Because of that reality, they need to see Jesus in how we live our everyday lives.

As it turns out, I was my Father's last chance to truly know Jesus.

My dad passed away from a drug overdose on the very same day I was hosting a men's conference. The timing of his death has left a lasting imprint on the importance of what we are called to do. Ministering to men is of the utmost importance. Our objective is not just to host events but to deal with the real issues men go through and prepare them to do what God has called them to do with the strength that He provides.

I had invited him to the conference, and he had shown interest in coming, but life with him was always difficult. He was hard to deal with, and the thought of managing his logistics and all the drama that comes with his issues related to drugs and character flaws felt like too much to deal with. It meant arranging a ride and setting him up in a hotel. Everything just felt overwhelming, especially with all the other responsibilities of the conference. I had a lot on my plate, and, in hindsight, I didn't ask for help in dealing with him the way I should have. This is why we need brothers to carry one another's burdens and help each other. We need to be able to call upon people for help when we need it.

I live with this, knowing that even though I was the nicest person in the family to him, I sometimes wondered if I was supposed to do more. I've processed this over time, and it has shaped my hunger to push men hard to step up and be living examples for those around them. It is the reason why I felt the need to write this book and inspire men to live up to the calling, no matter how difficult, no matter how overwhelming, no matter what we're going through.

Our mission is life or death. I thank God for His goodness because this story does have a happy ending.

About a month before his death, something incredible happened. He came to one of my church services, which was rare. That day, I preached a sermon on forgiveness, and for the first time, my father walked down the aisle, broken and weeping. He gave his life to the Lord that day. I had the privilege of praying with him, leading him to Jesus. I'll never forget seeing him standing there, in tears, in front of the congregation, fully surrendering to God. He kept crying after the service, telling me and all who would listen that he had never felt anything like that before. He had always had a form of faith in his own made-up version of the God he said he followed, but this was a real, genuine transformation.

> **We don't have time to leave things unsaid or delay what God calls us to do.**

That moment gave me peace because I believe with all my heart that he truly surrendered his life to God. I know I'll see him again in heaven. Even with that peace, I can't help but wonder how different things might have been if he had made it to the men's conference instead of being alone at home, falling back into old habits. It's a harsh reminder of how urgent this mission is—men need tangible examples of Jesus in their lives. The gospel isn't just a message; it's life or death. I really can't say that enough. I'll say it more urgently: It's not just life and death. It's eternal life and eternal separation and death.

My dad was finally trying to change but ran out of time. His death taught me something important: we don't have time to leave things unsaid or delay what God calls us to do. We have to be like Jesus now. We must make the most of every moment and live like He commands. As 1 John 2:3-6 (NIV) says:

> *We know that we have come to know him if we keep his commands. Whoever says, "I know him," but does not do what he commands is a liar, and the truth is not in that person. But if anyone obeys his Word, love for God is truly made complete in them. This is how we know we are in him: Whoever claims to live in him must live as Jesus did.*

John's words hit hard because they don't allow for half-hearted Christianity. They call for a life fully devoted to following Jesus—living as He lived, loving as He loved, and obeying as He obeyed.

That hard truth isn't about perfection or always doing things perfectly but a reminder about the direction of our lives. Are we truly striving to be like Jesus?

If you're up for it, read the rest of 1 John 1. Better yet, read the whole book—it's short but powerful. When you read it, you'll see a clear picture of what it means to be a faithful follower of Christ. And who better to tell us than John, the disciple who was one of the closest to Jesus's heart?

When we strive to be like Jesus, it's not just about mimicking His miracles or teachings. It reflects His love, humility, and obedience to the Father. Being like Jesus means becoming more like Him in our character, not just in our actions. It's about developing the same heart for God and for the people that He had.

BARRIERS TO BEING LIKE JESUS

1) Pride

Pride is one of the biggest obstacles to being like Jesus because it closes our eyes to our need for God and others. Jesus modeled humility; we must let go of our pride to be like Him.

"God opposes the proud but gives grace to the humble" (James 4:6).

2) Selfishness

Jesus was selfless, always putting others first. We live in a world that promotes self-gratification and self-advancement, but to be like Jesus, we must deny ourselves and live for others.

"If anyone would come after me, let him deny himself and take up his cross and follow me" (Matthew 16:24, ESV).

3) Fear

Fear of failure, rejection, or loss of control can prevent us from stepping into the life God has for us. Jesus faced every fear and hardship with faith and the truth of the Word. To be like Him, we must do the same.

"For God has not given us a spirit of fear, but of power, love, and self-discipline" (2 Timothy 1:7).

PRACTICAL STEPS TO BECOMING MORE LIKE JESUS

1) Spend Time with Him

Just as we become like the people we spend the most time with, we become more like Jesus when we spend time in His presence through prayer, worship, and reading the Word.

2) Seek to Serve, Not to Be Served

Jesus came to serve, and we are called to follow His example. Look for opportunities to serve others, even in small ways.

"For even the Son of Man did not come to be served, but to serve" (Mark 10:45, NIV).

3) Stay Connected to the Vine

Jesus said that we can't do anything apart from Him, and the more connected we are to Him, the more we will bear fruit in our lives.

"I am the vine; you are the branches. If you remain in me and I in you, you will bear much fruit" (John 15:5, NIV).

LIVE TO GLORIFY GOD

The Bible says, "No one has ever seen God. But if we love each other, God lives in us, and his love is brought to full expression in us" (1 John 4:12). This verse captures our ultimate calling as men—to reveal God through our love and actions. People may not see God directly, but through us, they can experience His presence. Directing people to Jesus is not a heavy burden; it lifts us with a sense of divine purpose. We have the incredible privilege of glorifying God in every area of our lives.

We glorify God through our work. As the Bible says, "Work willingly at whatever you do, as though you were working for the Lord rather than for people" (Colossians 3:23). This verse reminds us that no matter what our job or role, we ultimately serve God, and our diligence and integrity in our work reflect His nature.

We glorify God in our families, as "For a husband is the head of his wife as Christ is the head of the church. He is the Savior of his body, the church" (Ephesians 5:23). This verse shows the gravity of men's role in their families, called to lead as Christ leads—sacrificially and with love. Being like Jesus in our homes means putting others first and leading with humility and grace.

> **Even if you don't mean much to the world, you can mean the world to someone.**

We glorify God in our ministry, knowing that Jesus said, "I tell you the truth, anyone who believes in me will do the same works I have done, and even greater works, because I am going to be with the Father" (John 14:12). This verse calls us to a higher purpose in serving others, showing that we are empowered to continue His mission on earth, with the Holy Spirit guiding us to do even more than we could ever imagine.

If you feel insignificant or unimportant, that couldn't be further from the truth. You may never be famous or have millions of followers, and people may not write books about your life or achievements. Even if you don't mean much to the world, you can mean the world to someone. No matter how small your circle of influence may seem, your life has an immense impact when you live like Christ.

Men, you hold value; you hold significance because you carry the presence of God through His Holy Spirit. "Do you not know that your bodies are temples of the Holy Spirit, who is in you, whom you have received from God?" (1 Corinthians 6:19, NIV). Through your relationship with Jesus, you carry His presence wherever you go. Do your part in showing the world who Jesus is—start with your home, immediate circle, workplace, and those closest to you.

Take seriously the role you've been given, even if it feels insignificant. "God has given each of you a gift from his great variety of spiritual gifts. Use them well to serve one another" (1 Peter 4:10). When you use whatever gift you have, relying on God's strength, you will see how He can transform your life and the lives of those around you.

Work through each target area to become more Christ-like in your everyday life, and watch how God will use your efforts to change your world. As you walk this journey of faith, growing closer to Jesus, you will find that you are making a far more significant difference than you ever thought possible.

MEASUREMENT CHECK
AM I BECOMING MORE LIKE JESUS?

This self-assessment focuses on self-reflection, not perfection. It helps you identify growth areas as you strive to become more like Christ. For each question, rate yourself:

Fully Reflecting Christ: I feel confident that I reflect Jesus consistently in this area.

Needs Attention: I see areas where I can improve and know specific steps.

Not Reflecting Christ: I struggle in this area and must focus on growing here.

1) Christ-Like Love

Question: Do I love others as Jesus loves, putting their needs above mine, even when they are complex?

- Measurement: Reflect on how you treat people—your family, friends, coworkers, and strangers. Do you show grace, patience, and unconditional love, or do you become easily frustrated or selfish?
- Self-Check: Remember John 13:34-35: "So now I am giving you a new commandment: Love each other. Just as I have loved you, you should love each other. Your love for one another will prove to the world that you are my disciples." Christ-like love is sacrificial and requires us to put others first.

2) Humility and Service

Question: Am I serving others as Jesus did, humbly and without seeking recognition?

- Measurement: Think about how you approach service. Are you serving for recognition or self-gain, or are you humbly serving others, even when it goes unnoticed?
- Self-Check: Reflect on Mark 10:45: "For even the Son of Man came not to be served but to serve others and to give his life as a ransom for many." Serving like Jesus means seeking opportunities to help others without the need for acknowledgment.

3) Obedience to God

Question: Do I obey God's commands even when it's challenging or inconvenient?

- Measurement: Look at how you respond when God calls you to do something that's difficult or requires sacrifice. Do you resist, or do you obey Him with faith?
- Self-Check: Consider 1 John 2:3-6 (NIV): "We know that we have come to know him if we keep his commands. Whoever says, 'I know him,' but does not do what he commands is a liar, and the truth is not in that person. But if anyone obeys his Word, love for God is truly made complete in them." True discipleship means living in obedience to God's Word, even when it costs us something.

4) Compassion and Forgiveness

Question: Do I show compassion and forgive as Jesus forgives, or do I hold onto bitterness and grudges?

- Measurement: Reflect on your relationships. Are there people you struggle to forgive or show compassion to? Jesus forgave even those who wronged Him—do you follow His example?
- Self-Check: Ephesians 4:32 says, "Instead, be kind to each other, tenderhearted, forgiving one another, just as God through Christ has forgiven you." True Christ-likeness involves showing the same mercy and forgiveness that we have received from Him.

5) Trust in God's Plan

Question: Do I trust God's plan for my life, even when it doesn't make sense or when I face challenges?

- Measurement: In moments of uncertainty or difficulty, do you find yourself doubting God's plan, or do you trust Him fully, knowing He is in control?
- Self-Check: Reflect on Proverbs 3:5-6: "Trust in the LORD with all your heart; do not depend on your own understanding. Seek his will in all you do, and he will show you which path to take." Trusting God means letting go of the need to control everything and placing your life in His hands.

Scoring the Maturity Check

1) Fully Reflecting Christ: You are consistently growing in areas such as love, humility, obedience, and trust.

2) Needs Attention: You see where you need growth but may struggle with consistency. Identify specific areas to work on and make a plan for progress.

3) Not Reflecting Christ: You're finding it difficult to embrace key aspects of Christ-likeness. Take time to seek God's guidance, asking for strength to make small but meaningful changes.

NEXT STEPS:
- If you scored "Fully Reflecting Christ": Keep pressing forward! Continue to deepen your walk with God and serve as a model for others.
- If you scored "Needs Attention": Choose one or two areas to focus on and make small, intentional changes in those areas.
- If you scored "Not Reflecting Christ": Don't be discouraged. Ask God for guidance and begin by addressing one area

where you need growth. You don't have to tackle everything at once—just take one step toward being more like Jesus.

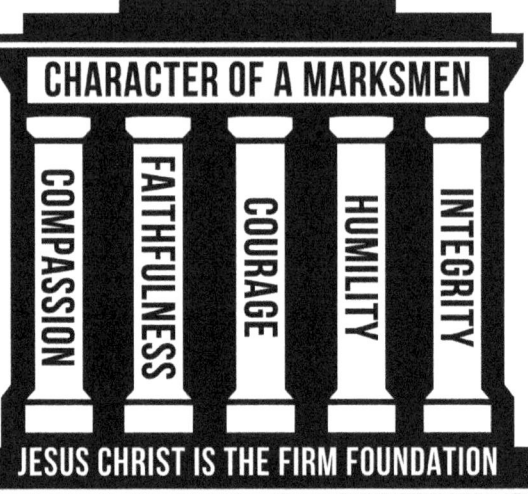

PART 3
THE CHARACTER OF A MARKSMAN

Hitting the target every now and then is one thing, but hitting it daily is an entirely different challenge. To grow in our walk with God and consistently live out our faith, we must take a serious inventory of our character. Character is proven and tested over time. Your gifts and talents might open doors, create opportunities, or even help you build friendships and relationships, but it's your character that will keep you there. You will never have meaningful relationships or long-term success without addressing your character. Anyone can pretend to be something for a short period, but only men of high character can sustain it long-term.

This final section will discuss the five pillars that uphold marksmens' character—integrity, humility, courage, faithfulness, and compassion. These are active character traits that we must understand and live out daily so that others will see our good works and give glory to God. Jesus emphasizes this principle in Matthew 5:16: "In the same way, let your good deeds shine out for all to see so that everyone will praise your heavenly Father." Our character is meant to shine through our actions, giving honor to God in all we do. These five pillars are the foundation that holds up our character as marksmen. When we master

these traits, we become like a strong house, able to withstand life's challenges and remain firm. Paul reminds us in 1 Corinthians 3:11: "For no one can lay any foundation other than the one we already have—Jesus Christ." It is up to us to build upon that foundation

with strength and godly character.

Over the years, I've experienced growth and success in my personal life and business by

striving to embody these character traits. Now, I want to teach other men the value of these principles. You have learned the way of the marksman, you have understood the measure of a marksman, and now it's time to evaluate the character of the marksman. Let's dive into these five pillars, which will be the lasting legacy you leave behind as a man of God.

CHAPTER 10
MEN OF INTEGRITY

Integrity is the quality of upholding honesty and strong principles. It involves consistency in actions, values, and outcomes, even when no one is watching. The Bible says, "The integrity of the upright guides them, but the unfaithful are destroyed by their duplicity" (Proverbs 11:3, NIV). This verse speaks to the idea that integrity guides us and protects us from the destruction caused by dishonesty or deceit. People with integrity are known for being trustworthy and standing firm in their beliefs, regardless of external pressures or temptations.

I've built a long-trusted career in business because people know they can count on me to be open and honest in every deal. I've been involved in multimillion-dollar projects that directly impact society. When people do business with me, they know they get upfront, truthful interactions. I've known other businesspeople who may get ahead, make more money, or succeed through dishonesty, but in the end, that will mean nothing when we stand before a Holy God. God has blessed me with more than just material gain because I've made it my goal to be a man of integrity in my life and business dealings.

Of course, being a man of integrity is necessary in every area of life, not just business. I want to share some real-life examples of the effects. I've been a salesman since I was nineteen, and early on, I was told to "do whatever it takes" to get an order—even if it meant bending the truth. Lying, or, as they put it, "just a little white lie," didn't sit right with me. I chose to do business my way, following my faith and values. I wanted a business mind but a ministry heart, and I wasn't okay with dishonesty. Looking back, I believe with all my heart that this is why God has blessed my endeavors.

> **I can't stress this enough: Integrity is always about doing the right thing, even when no one is watching.**

I can't stress this enough: **Integrity is always about doing the right thing, even when no one is watching.** Most people live life focusing on getting away with as much as possible. A man of God has character and lives a life that aligns with biblical values, even when difficult or uncomfortable. As a teenager, when I worked at AMC Theatres, God challenged me to treat my job as if I were the owner. That meant no more long breaks or sneaking free popcorn to my friends or pretty girls. Walking with integrity, like I owned the place, would be my first test of transformation—from being broke and heading nowhere to becoming a success story—the beginning of my journey from a high school dropout to a business owner.

I was seventeen years old, running my role as a supervisor with a sense of responsibility. For the first time in my life, I took responsibility seriously, not from external pressure but from the inspiration that came from within by the Spirit of God. That transformational shift started long before I owned a business; it began when I was making $5 an hour. Being a man of integrity has nothing to do with your position. Whether you're the boss or the entry-level worker, it's about doing things right, no matter the cost. What started off small became a principle I lived by and evolved into a core value and essential part of my business success.

God put my character to the test in more ways than one. At the time, it was particularly bad at home; I had no money for food. I had to help pay the bills, and one day, I found a wallet with over $1,000 cash. I turned it in. Turning that much money in was hard, especially since I had a real need. My sisters were counting on me. My mom was counting on me as my dad was in jail. Even though I was only seventeen years old, I had real pressure. There was even a part of me who thought God was answering my prayers and blessing me to meet my needs. Nobody would know that I found it. I had been a Christian for less than a year, and I did not know any better. The old me would've kept that money, but God was building character. The guy who came looking for it hours later was upset, thinking for sure that someone had taken the cash. I honestly thought that man would be so grateful that all the money was in his wallet. I thought he would give me something, but he didn't reward me or even say thank you after they told him a teenager had found his wallet and turned it in. I know now that God's reward for me wasn't temporary relief from being broke. My reward was the integrity God was building in me so that He could bless me over the long term.

Integrity means facing difficult situations head-on.

That is why, at nineteen, I would not lie or cheat to make a deal. God had already reformed my character. I know God's work in me as a teenager at the AMC movie theater was preparation, so by the time I started my company at twenty-six, we took off right from the start.

Integrity means facing difficult situations head-on. Men of integrity don't run from bad situations and are not afraid to have hard conversations.

It's easy to share good news, but true integrity shows when you're willing to have hard conversations, even when the news is terrible. Those who succeed don't run from difficult tasks; they handle them directly and honestly.

I don't always make the right decisions, and life doesn't always go according to plan. But a man of integrity owns up to his mistakes and tells the truth, even when it's hard. Proverbs 10:9 says, "People with integrity walk safely, but those who follow crooked paths will be exposed." This verse reminds us that a man of integrity walks with confidence and security, knowing his actions align with God's truth.

While our gifts and talents may open doors, our integrity keeps those doors open. People do business again with me even when things go wrong because they know I'll do whatever it takes to make things right. For me, business came easy—relationships didn't. People are more complex, and being direct and brutally honest can sometimes backfire.

Integrity is more than brutal honesty; it's about being compassionate, trustworthy, and standing firm in your beliefs, regardless of external pressures or temptations. It means being someone people can count on. Jesus Himself said, "Let your yes be yes, and your no be no" (Matthew 5:37, author paraphrase). This verse explains the value of being dependable so your words hold value; it's crucial in relationships, whether it's with family, friends, or colleagues. Relationships are emotionally complex, and integrity means being reliable, compassionate, and transparent, even when life is complicated.

Trust in Relationships: Integrity builds trust in relationships. Your spouse, children, or friends must know they can count on you to be truthful, dependable, and consistent. Trust isn't established overnight; it's developed through honesty and reliability over time. When you live with integrity, your relationships will deepen because people will see that you are the same person behind closed doors as in public.

Family Life: In family relationships, integrity means leading by example. As a husband and father, your children will learn from watching you. They need to see that you're a man of your word and that you live with integrity, even when no one is watching. Proverbs 20:7 reminds us, "The godly walk with integrity; blessed are their children who follow them." Integrity has a ripple effect—it blesses not only your life but the lives of those who follow your example.

PRACTICAL STEPS FOR LIVING WITH INTEGRITY

1) Consistency

Be consistent in your actions, whether people are watching or not. Let your yes be yes, and your no be no. In both business and relationships, people need to know they can trust your word and that you will follow through.

2) Accountability

Surround yourself with people who will hold you accountable to your commitments and values. Whether it's a mentor, a close friend, or a spouse, accountability keeps us on the right path.

3) Transparency

Be honest about your struggles and work through them with God's help. No one is perfect, but admitting your mistakes and taking steps to correct them builds trust and respect.

INTEGRITY ISN'T OPTIONAL

Let integrity be a core part of who you are. Make that character trait one of your top priorities.

> **Too many of us are content with being somewhat reliable, but as men striving to reflect Christ, we must aim higher.**

Take a moment to search your heart and ask yourself: *What kind of man do I want to be? Do I want to be someone people can rely on? Do I leave people wondering, hoping for the best, like rolling dice in Vegas?* This may seem like a big swing from one end to the other, but a half-truth is not the truth. When it comes to integrity, it's all or nothing. Too many of us are content with being somewhat reliable, but as men striving to reflect Christ, we must aim higher.

I understand that we often act with good intentions. Still, as marksmen, we must go beyond good intentions. We must be deliberate, pointed, and intentional in upholding our character. We are ambassadors of Christ, and when people see us, they should see Jesus. They should see a man of consistency and reliability. We are not just representing ourselves; we are representing the truth that Jesus revealed in His Word. As His followers and His body, we must live in a way that brings honor to His name by being men that people can count on and who live out the truth, no matter the circumstances.

Personal Challenge:

Take time this week to evaluate your actions. Are you being consistent in your integrity? Identify one area where you may need to grow in trustworthiness or consistency, whether in your business dealings, relationships, or personal commitments. Set a goal to be more intentional about living with integrity in that area. Write it down and ask someone you trust to help hold you accountable as you work toward becoming a man others can depend on.

CHAPTER 11
MEN OF HUMILITY

Humility is often misunderstood in our culture, especially regarding men. It's not about being weak or diminishing our view of ourselves; it's about being able to look honestly at who we are, why we are doing what we are doing, and measuring that against the old saying, "What would Jesus do?" Jesus Himself was humble and took the stature of a servant. True humility is understanding that all we have—from our talents and resources to our successes—are gifts from God. To live as a man of God, practicing humility is necessary. The Bible teaches us, "God opposes the proud but gives grace to the humble" (James 4:6), and He exalts those who humble themselves before Him (James 4:10). Humility means acknowledging that our importance is limited, especially in comparison to God. A man who embraces humility rejects arrogance and pride, recognizing his limitations and valuing others above himself.

> In the Bible, humility is not about thinking less of yourself but rather thinking of yourself less.

Humility requires self-awareness and a biblical perspective of what it means to be humble. Many men have perfected the "humble brag," projecting a false sense of humility, but we should approach humility from a biblical point of view. That starts with recognizing one's utter dependency on God and placing God's will and the care of others above personal desires. Those personal traits require us to submit to God, acknowledge our human limitations regardless of our success, and serve others—viewing them as valuable, in some cases, more valuable than oneself. Philippians 2:3-4 instructs, "Don't be selfish; don't try to impress others. Be humble, thinking of others as better than yourselves. Don't look out only for your own interests, but take an interest in others, too." James 4:10 advises, "Humble yourselves before the Lord, and he will lift you up in honor." Micah 6:8 clarifies, "O people, the LORD has told you what is good, and this is what he requires of you: to do what is right, to love mercy, and to walk humbly with your God."

In the Bible, humility is not about thinking less of yourself but rather thinking of yourself less, focusing more on God's purpose and the needs of others.

Humility isn't something that came naturally to me. I've always been driven and competitive—sometimes to a fault. I thrive when people tell me I can't do something; it lights a fire in me. Early in my life, negative reinforcement was my fuel—it was me against the world. I carried a chip on my shoulder, always trying to prove people wrong. In some ways, it worked for me. I broke into the electronics industry during the .com crash and survived despite the odds. I started my business in the middle of the 2008 housing crisis, and even though it wasn't ideal, we pushed through. At one point, I nearly lost everything, but by God's grace, we made it through.

That same mentality drove me when I stepped into my role as lead pastor in 2020, during the COVID-19 global pandemic, when we couldn't even meet for services. Challenges like that don't scare me; if anything, they motivate me. But through all this, I've learned the hard way that my biggest enemy isn't the circumstances I face—it's my own pride.

My drive and ambition often blur the line between healthy competition and unhealthy pride. I've realized that the same mindset that helped me push through tough times also turned into arrogance and stubbornness when left unchecked. I got so good at seeing the negatives—doubters and critics—that I started seeing shadows where there were none. This attitude affected my relationships; I would look for trouble, even where it didn't exist. I became so focused on proving people wrong that I forgot to enjoy the positives in life.

> **Anyone can be humble when they're in the gutter—it's on the mountaintop that humility is the hardest.**

Here's the thing about pride: God will humble you when you least expect it. Trust me on that. It's easy to be humble when you've got nothing. We Christians tend to call on God when we're at our lowest and need Him the most. But when things are going well, that's when we're most vulnerable to pride. We think we've figured it all out, and we start leaving God out of the equation. That's when we set ourselves up for a fall. *Anyone can be humble when they're in the gutter—it's on the mountaintop that humility is the hardest.*

Please take my advice: *learn humility in every season.* Don't wait for God to humble you. Trust me, He can, and He will if needed. But it's far better to live with a mindset of humility before you're forced to learn that lesson the hard way.

HUMILITY IN MINISTRY: A LESSON FROM THE PLATFORM

In business, I got away with my pride for a while. But in ministry, God wouldn't let me off the hook so easily. I knew I couldn't rely on my own strength.

When I took over the church in 2020, we had this ugly green carpet on the platform. It drove me crazy for years, and I always said, "The first thing I'll do if I ever become lead pastor is get rid of that carpet!" So, naturally, during the pandemic shutdowns, even though we had no money, I just took over. We couldn't even meet in the building. I could not help myself, even though it may have been unwise. I tore up the carpet, and we trusted God to provide the funds for a replacement.

As we ripped it up, we found handwritten notes, Bible verses, and prayers from the congregation in the late '80s when they built the stage. It was a humbling moment, and instead of making this a "me" project, we invited the church family to contribute again. Everyone who gave was invited to write a note or verse on the platform for future generations.

But here's the part that really hit me. On the last day, as we prepared to cover the platform, I realized I hadn't written anything.

I prayed, and in that moment, God humbled me again. I wrote "Jesus 1st" right at the front of the platform. That reminder is there every time I stand to preach. *No matter how creative or successful we become, this platform—and this ministry—belong to Jesus.*

It was a real reminder that "unless the LORD builds the house, the builders labor in vain" (Psalm 127:1, NIV). Our long-term success isn't going to come from my ideas or drive—it's going to come from staying humble and putting Jesus first.

1) Acknowledge Your Limitations

Humility starts by recognizing that we are not self-sufficient. Reflect on how dependent you are on God's grace and strength. This will help you see your accomplishments through the lens of gratitude, not pride.

2) Put Others First

Actively look for ways to prioritize the needs of others above your own. Whether in your family, workplace, or church, practice valuing others by listening, serving, and showing empathy.

3) Seek Feedback

Invite others to speak into your life. Be open to criticism and correction. This requires vulnerability but also accelerates growth in humility.

4) Stay Grateful

Make gratitude a daily practice. Recognize the ways God has blessed you, and give thanks for those blessings, knowing they are not of your own doing but a gift from Him.

PERSONAL CHALLENGE:

Humility isn't just a trait we develop during tough times. Are you practicing humility when things are going well? Take time to examine areas where pride may be creeping in. Are you willing to admit your weaknesses and seek God's strength? Remember that God gives grace to the humble (James 4:6). Don't wait for God to humble you—walk in humility now, both in the valley and on the mountaintop.

KEY BIBLE VERSES ON HUMILITY:

1) **Philippians 2:3-4 (NIV):** "Do nothing out of selfish ambition or vain conceit. Rather, in humility value others above yourselves, not looking to your own interests but each of you to the interests of the others."
2) **James 4:10 (NIV):** "Humble yourselves before the Lord, and he will lift you up."
3) **Micah 6:8 (ESV):** "He has told you, O man, what is good; and what does the LORD require of you but to do justice, and to love kindness, and to walk humbly with your God?"

CHAPTER 12
MEN OF COURAGE

Courage is required of marksmen. In today's world, courage is often described as bravery when applied to men. I believe that is an oversimplification. We hear that men should stand firm in the face of danger when others are scared. We are taught men should not show fear, act tough, or fight in battle. All these things are good and not wrong, but we need to go deeper.

Biblical courage is much more than that. It's about doing what is right and living out God's Word, standing your ground on moral and spiritual principles, and not compromising even when life is challenging. As Paul teaches in Romans 12:2: "Don't copy the behavior and customs of this world but let God transform you into a new person by changing the way you think." Biblical courage means standing firm and being willing to go against the grain when everyone else conforms to the patterns of the world. It's allowing God to change the way you think, aligning your thoughts with His thoughts.

Change is one of the hardest and scariest things to do in this life. God's plan for us is to be transformed into His likeness, not just His image. We are all born in His image, but we only reflect His glory when we are courageous enough to follow Him and be transformed into His likeness. The difference between being in his likeness and being born into His image is that while we all bear God's image through qualities like reason, love, and free will, living in His likeness is a deliberate journey of spiritual growth. It involves embracing His character, aligning our thoughts and actions with Christ's example, and letting God's power shape us according to His love and holiness. We can't settle and be content staying where we are. If we want to be more Christ-like, we must have the courage to challenge ourselves.

Our courage as men of God will be tested. We have to ask ourselves: will we stand firm, or will we compromise our values? You will be put in situations that require hard decisions, and making those decisions will feel scary. Uncertain outcomes add to the weight of our choices, and if we are not careful, we can let fear grab a hold of us. Sooner or later, you will have to face and overcome your own fears. As a *Star Wars* nerd, I'm reminded of what Luke Skywalker said: "Confronting fear is the destiny of a Jedi."[8] Confronting fear also rings true for us. Fear is a powerful tool of the enemy and an influential emotion, causing even mighty men to turn from their purpose and conform to external pressures instead of God's truth. Fear brings doubt, and with doubt comes uncertainty. When you're uncertain, you become double-minded, and as Scripture warns, "A double-minded man should not expect to receive anything from the Lord" (James 1:7-8, author paraphrase). How can you move forward in faith and be unsure simultaneously? Chances are, you will freeze, give up, or compromise.

There have been many moments when I had to face my own fears and doubts, and the courage I found in God's Word helped me push through. Joshua 1:9 reminds us: "This is my

---
8   J.J. Abrams, *Star Wars: The Rise of Skywalker* (December 16, 2019; Burbank: Walt Disney) Dolby Theater.

command—be strong and courageous! Do not be afraid or discouraged. For the LORD your God is with you wherever you go."

Through courage, we find the strength to see God's promises fulfilled—not just for ourselves but for our families, our churches, and our communities. A man who acts with courage can inspire everyone around him. Notice how this is a command given to Joshua—because biblical courage requires an act of obedience.

Running from difficult situations only makes things worse.

One of the great joys of fatherhood is how children look up to you when they're young. It's often said that all boys see their fathers as heroes when they're little. However, as they become teenagers, their perspective shifts. I saw my dad as strong and capable, but as I grew older, I realized he struggled to confront his fears. He ran from responsibility and avoided the tough decisions that could have changed his life. It soured our relationship—it hurt him when I distanced myself from him in those years, which caused him to go deeper into his drug and destructive behavior. Running from difficult situations only makes things worse. Children view things through a pure lens, but as we mature, we see things for what they are. You can pretend to be strong, but people will eventually see through it if you consistently live in fear.

I began to reflect on the kind of man I wanted to be—a man of courage rooted not only in the Word of God but empowered by the Spirit of God. I want to be a man my children and congregation can look up to, confident in the Lord and unafraid to take challenging, faithful steps.

Throughout the Bible, we see examples of people who demonstrated courage and obedience. Daniel continued praying despite the king's decree. Esther risked her life to save her people. David stood before Goliath with nothing but faith. The disciples spread the gospel despite persecution. The Bible is full of men and women just like us—human and flawed—but courageous in obeying God's call.

FACING GIANTS, FACING CHANGE

Joshua's story is one of the clearest examples of courage in the Bible. Imagine taking over for Moses, the man who led Israel through the wilderness and delivered them out of Egypt. Joshua had a massive responsibility: to lead the people into the Promised Land—a land full of giants and obstacles. Joshua 1:5-7, God told Joshua:

> "No one will be able to stand against you as long as you live. For I will be with you as I was with Moses. I will not fail you or abandon you. Be strong and courageous, for you are the one who will lead these people to possess all the land I swore to their ancestors I would give them. Be strong and very courageous. Be careful to obey all the instructions Moses gave you. Do not deviate from them, turning either to the right or to the left. Then you will be successful in everything you do."

Joshua wasn't just facing an external challenge—he had to lead a new generation of Israelites who had only known struggle and the wilderness. Like Joshua, we're often called to step into new challenges, face our own "giants," and lead others where they haven't gone before. And just like Joshua, we have God's assurance that He will not fail or abandon us.

The story of Joshua teaches us the power of courage. To be men of courage, we must live by faith over fear, obeying God without wavering in the face of challenges. We must value personal devotion and study to understand the direction courage will lead us, ultimately bringing us to success and prosperity. Joshua's journey into the Promised Land provides powerful inspiration for the type of men we need to become. The first generation of Israelites failed to enter the Promised Land because they were afraid. They saw the giants and let fear drive their decisions. But God calls us to be strong and courageous. He wants us to trust Him, even when the obstacles seem insurmountable. As men of God, we face moments where we must choose between faith and fear. The difference between success and failure lies in our willingness to step forward in faith. Let's dig deeper into this story.

Obey Without Wavering

In Joshua 1:7, God commands Joshua to obey everything Moses taught him without deviation: "Be careful to obey all the instructions Moses gave you. Do not deviate from them, turning either to the right or to the left. Then you will be successful in everything you do." This command wasn't just about bravery but about unwavering obedience to God's Word.

Our success and victory are not determined by our strength alone but by our obedience to what we've learned from God.

When life gets hard, it's tempting to look for shortcuts or to stray from the teachings and principles that God has set before us. However, true courage is found in standing firm in God's Word, even when the path is difficult. We cannot waver, even in times of weariness or discouragement. Our success and victory are not determined by our strength alone but by our obedience to what we've learned from God.

Joshua's story illustrates that his success wasn't simply a matter of bravery or military strategy; it was deeply rooted in his obedience to God's clear instructions. Throughout the biblical narrative of entering the Promised Land, it becomes clear that Joshua's victories were not achieved by courage alone but through unwavering obedience and dependency on God. This teaches us that courage without obedience is incomplete, and true victory comes when we rely on God's strength and His direction for our lives.

Personal Devotion and Study

Joshua 1:8 gives us another key to living with courage: "Study this Book of Instruction continually. Meditate on it day and night so you will be sure to obey everything written in it. Only then will you prosper and succeed in all you do."

Personal devotion and study of God's Word are essential. It's not enough to hear it from others—we need to know it for ourselves. In these quiet moments with God, we courageously face life's battles. True courage comes from a deep connection with God through prayer, study, and meditation on His Word.

Success and Prosperity

Finally, God promises in Joshua 1:9, "This is my command—be strong and courageous! Do not be afraid or discouraged. For the LORD your God is with you wherever you go."

This isn't just encouragement—it's a command. Fear is not an option, and neither is turning back. We are called to move forward in faith, with the assurance that God is with us. When we trust Him, obey Him, and seek Him with all our hearts, we will not only succeed but prosper in everything we do.

CHALLENGE: EMBRACE COURAGE

In your life, you will face battles, challenges, and new seasons that require courage. Are you ready to step into those moments with faith? God has called you to be a man of courage, to stand firm even when the odds seem overwhelming. As you reflect on Joshua's journey, ask yourself:

- Where is God asking me to be courageous in this season?
- How can I strengthen my faith and trust God in the battles ahead?

Be strong, be courageous, and remember that God is with you wherever you go.

The key to biblical courage is obedience—following God's instructions no matter the situation. Courage in the Bible goes beyond just bravery; it involves a deep trust in God's plan and the willingness to act on it, even when the outcome is uncertain or risky.

Risk is not the measure of courage, but it will almost certainly be part of the journey.

If more men sought to understand God's plan for their lives and had the courage to follow through, we would see a transformation in our world. I wish I could say I've always been courageous in every situation, but I haven't. However, when I've taken calculated risks, trusting in God, He has always been faithful. Risk is not the measure of courage, but it will almost certainly be part of the journey. Jesus told His disciples, "I am sending you out as sheep among wolves" (Matthew 10:16), warning them that following Him would come with inherent risks.

Jesus also emphasized counting the cost of discipleship, saying, "But don't begin until you count the cost" (Luke 14:28). This verse reminds us that biblical courage isn't about reckless action—it involves prayerful discernment and calculated steps of faith. Once you know the direction God is calling you to, it's a matter of being faithful, obedient, and courageous. You will notice in this book that some of the same verses are repeated in different chapters because they apply to so many circumstances in life.

Micah 6:8 offers profound wisdom on this matter, highlighting three essential qualities that build the foundation for courage:

1) Do What Is Right (Justice)

Live with integrity and stand up for what is just, even when it is difficult. Courage calls us to act on the side of truth and justice, no matter the consequences.

2) Love Mercy

True courage also involves showing compassion and kindness when holding grudges or retaliating is easier. Mercy takes strength and bravery, as it goes against the grain of our pride.

3) Walk Humbly With Your God

Humility is the key to courage. It means recognizing our dependence on God and acknowledging that we can't do it alone. Courage comes from walking humbly before God, trusting Him to lead us in every situation.

As shown in Joshua's story, courage and obedience are woven throughout Scripture: "Be strong and courageous! Do not be afraid or discouraged. For the LORD your God is with you wherever you go" (Joshua 1:9). Courage and obedience go hand in hand, and God's instructions are clear: trust Him, follow His Word, and He will be with you through every challenge.

Faith requires courage, and courage in God's kingdom means more than just bravery in battle—it's about trusting God's will, obeying His Word, and moving forward with bold faith. As men of God, people should look at us and see men who are confident in the Lord and willing to trust Him through every season of life.

PRACTICAL APPLICATION
COURAGE IN ACTION

Biblical courage is not just a concept; it's a practice that must be applied daily. Here are a few ways to build and exercise courage in your life:

1) **Face Your Fears With Faith:** Identify areas in your life where fear holds you back. Is it fear of failure, rejection, or the unknown? Instead of retreating, bring those fears before

God in prayer. Remember, "For God has not given us a spirit of fear and timidity, but of power, love, and self-discipline" (2 Timothy 1:7).

2) **Practice Obedience Even When It's Uncomfortable:** When God asks you to step out of your comfort zone, courage is often needed. Whether it's leading a Bible study, sharing your faith with a coworker, or making a tough decision in your family, practice obedience without hesitation. "Be strong and very courageous. Be careful to obey all the instructions. . . . Then you will be successful in everything you do" (Joshua 1:7).

3) **Build a Habit of Personal Devotion:** Strength comes from a close relationship with God. Make time for daily prayer and study of Scripture. Allow God's Word to speak to your heart and give you the courage to face whatever lies ahead. "Meditate on it [the Word] day and night so you will be sure to obey. . . . Only then will you prosper and succeed in all you do" (Joshua 1:8).

4) **Be a Role Model of Courage:** Whether you're a father, brother, or leader in your community, people are watching how you respond to life's challenges. Let them see a man of courage who stands firm in faith. Be the man who inspires others to trust God and walk in obedience, regardless of the obstacles.

5) **Trust God's Plan:** True courage comes from knowing that God is in control. Even when you can't see the outcome, trust that He has a purpose for every situation. As Romans 8:28 (BSB) teaches us, "God works all things together

for the good of those who love Him." Courage isn't about the absence of fear but choosing to trust God despite it.

6) **Ask Yourself:** Where is God asking you to be courageous right now? What fears do you need to confront with faith? How can you take a step of obedience today, trusting in God's promises?

CHAPTER 13
MEN OF COMPASSION

Now, we arrive at the next pillar of the character of marksmen, and I believe it is one of the most critical when striving to be more like Jesus: being men of compassion. Compassion is truly the heart of Jesus. Matthew 9:36 says, "When he saw the crowds, he had compassion on them because they were confused and helpless, like sheep without a shepherd." Jesus didn't look at the broken condition of people with frustration, anger, or irritation over their misguided beliefs. Instead, He was moved with compassion, so much so that He took action. This compassion is foundational to the mission of the church and our calling as men of God—to continue the work of Jesus by sending laborers and being laborers in the harvest field (Matthew 9:37-38).

What's even more striking is how Jesus reserved His harshest words for religious leaders who twisted God's Word, yet He remained compassionate toward those who were lost or struggling. This contrast teaches us that we, too, must maintain a heart of compassion when caring for others in need or who are lost while we stand firm against those who distort the truth.

BIBLICAL COMPASSION VS. HUMAN COMPASSION

If we're not careful, our hearts can lead us away from biblical compassion and, instead, toward a misguided form of compassion based on human emotion. Human compassion is often driven by emotions, social norms, or the desire to alleviate guilt. We see a bad situation, feel something, and may want to respond. This, in itself, is good. However, as Christ's followers, we have to go deeper than that. The motives that drive us to act determine whether our compassion is rooted in God's love or simply in our emotions.

Biblical compassion calls for sacrificial commitment and love and a willingness to serve others even when inconvenient or painful. Jesus Himself modeled this perfectly. Many men have compassion for the people within their circle, but how far does that compassion extend to strangers? How about one step further: How do you feel about those who get on your last nerve?

> **The person who is against you today can become your brother tomorrow.**

Today, many are divided over social issues, political views, and even differences in doctrine. These differences often stir up emotions that don't lead us toward compassionate witness but, instead, create anger, judgment, and division. It turns us against each other while a lost and broken world watches. As Jesus demonstrated, biblical compassion is not bound by such biases. Jesus said, "But I say, love your enemies! Pray for those who persecute you!"

(Matthew 5:44) His compassion was a radical departure from our usual way of thinking; His lifestyle and example challenge our very nature. God's character and compassion go beyond just reacting to the moment; they go beyond circumstances and beyond momentary actions like charitable giving or random acts of kindness. The person who is against you today can become your brother tomorrow. If you had met me before Christ, I was more likely to rob you than to lead you. He wants our hearts to be aligned with His. We need to know there is more at stake in how we treat people and how we respond to people. People need Him, and we are His hands and feet.

Jesus said, "Your love for one another will prove to the world that you are my disciples" (John 13:35). He didn't say this proof would come because we all voted the same way, thought the same, or dressed the same. Our compassion for those in need of a shepherd reveals where our hearts truly are. Our differences can make us better if we learn how to communicate with love and compassion. And even when we bring correction to a believer, we are reminded: "Dear brothers and sisters, if another believer is overcome by some sin, you who are godly should gently and humbly help that person back onto the right path. And be careful not to fall into the same temptation yourself" (Galatians 6:1).

Biblical compassion seeks to address both the physical and spiritual needs of others. While human compassion often seeks to alleviate immediate suffering, biblical compassion is aware of the eternal stakes. Jesus was moved by compassion to heal the sick and feed the hungry, but He also proclaimed the Good News of salvation, understanding that the deeper need was for eternal salvation.

In 1 John 3:17-18, we are reminded of the call to compassion: "If someone has enough money to live well and sees a brother or sister in need but shows no compassion—how can God's love be in that person? Dear children, let's not merely say that we love each other; let us show the truth by our actions." True compassion is not just a feeling; it's a call to action driven by God's love.

In summary, while both forms of compassion involve a response to suffering, biblical compassion is deeper. God's love seeks to serve others in a way that reflects the unconditional love of Christ. It is not about temporary relief but more about aligning our actions with God's eternal purposes.

That is the challenge: everything you've read in this book calls you to a higher purpose and a deeper relationship with God. It's about gaining more insight into your importance as a man of God. Why settle for where you are when you don't have to? God is ready to help you grow. At our church, we often say we want to move from our current state to God's desired state. There's always a distance between the person we are and the person we're striving to become, but the beautiful thing is that God is with you every step of the way.

> **True wealth comes from understanding how to be content with where you are yet willing to press forward toward something greater.**

Remember to have compassion for yourself no matter where you are on that journey. As men, we tend to be incredibly hard on ourselves. Yet, Jesus reminds us to love our neighbors as we love ourselves (Mark 12:31), and part of that commandment means learning to love ourselves in a healthy, Christ-centered way. In context, when Jesus was asked about the greatest commandment, He said: "Love the LORD your God with all your heart, all your soul, all your mind, and all your strength. The second is equally important: 'Love your neighbor as yourself.' There is no commandment greater than these" (Mark 12:30-31). This reminds us that every part of our walk with God should be compared to these two commandments—loving God fully and extending that same love to others, including ourselves.

When I reflect on my own journey, I often get frustrated. There's a part of me that's never fully satisfied, constantly critiquing myself for the things I'm not doing or haven't yet accomplished. But I've learned that constant self-criticism doesn't lead to growth. Paul was right when he said, "Godliness with contentment is itself great wealth" (1 Timothy 6:6). True wealth comes from understanding how to be content with where you are yet still willing to press forward toward something greater. When I think of this verse, I thank God that true wealth is found in His peace.

Through counseling, I realized that being hard on myself wasn't helping me become who God called me to be. We all get stuck in the "coulda, shoulda, woulda" mindset, but I remind myself that while I may have a long way to go to reach my goals, thank God I'm not where I used to be. Each step we take toward becoming more like Jesus is valuable and essential, no matter how small that step may seem. Be kind and compassionate to yourself as you grow in faith and character. God, who loves us completely, calls us to show the same grace and compassion to ourselves that we extend to others. Jesus taught us to pray, "Forgive us our sins, as we have forgiven those who sin against us" (Matthew 6:12). Love, grace, and compassion must be extended to ourselves and to others, not one or the other.

COMPASSION IN RELATIONSHIPS

Compassion should be at the heart of our relationships with family, friends, and even strangers. When applied in marriage, compassion can unlock the best in the relationship. When a man seeks to truly understand his wife's struggles and supports her emotional, physical, and spiritual needs, it's like hitting a home run in game seven of the World Series. It's a win for the relationship and glorifies God. Ephesians 5:25 (NIV) reminds us to "love your wives, just as Christ loved the church and gave himself up for her."

In friendships, compassion enables us to be present in others' lives, listening to their struggles and helping bear their burdens. Galatians 6:2 instructs us to "Share each other's burdens, and in this way obey the law of Christ."

Even in our communities and workplaces, compassion makes a tremendous impact. Showing kindness to a coworker during difficult times, helping a neighbor in need, or simply being present for someone who feels overlooked are all ways to reflect Christ's compassion in daily life. Jesus taught this when He said, "When I was hungry, you fed me; when I was cold, you clothed me" (Matthew 25:35, author paraphrase). His disciples were confused, so He explained: "Whatever you did for one of the least of these brothers and sisters of mine, you did for me" (Matthew 25:40, NIV).

Let that sink in: when we care for our wives, children, friends, strangers, and enemies, God sees it as living directly for Him. He not only sees the actions but the motives and the heart behind them. That's why 1 Peter 1:22 tells us, "Love each other deeply with all your heart." Don't just pretend to love—truly love others.

Living out genuine compassion through our strength is hard and sometimes impossible. This is why we must rely on the Holy Spirit to renew our minds and inspire our hearts daily. Compassion that is rooted in Christ's love doesn't just transform our close relationships; it has the power to change our entire community, city, and even the world. While women often seem more naturally in tune with emotional sensitivity, that does not mean compassion is reserved for them alone. Men are equally called to reflect Jesus's compassion, and this is something I've had to learn and grow in myself.

As I've hopefully expressed throughout this book, the things I write about didn't come quickly for me. God had to radically change my heart. I used to believe in tough love and straight talk—I was motivated by negatives and tried to project that onto my children. But it didn't work the way I expected. They didn't respond to the harshness the way I thought they would, and I realized that I needed to change my approach. I've always found it difficult to express affection and tenderness. Even today, I struggle with hugging people. It's ironic because we've created a church culture where everyone hugs, and I still feel uncomfortable with it. Still, I push through and do it anyway.

I can trace this discomfort back to my childhood. My dad would often be affectionate when he was high or drunk, usually after being abusive. He'd apologize, get emotional, and make us hug him. So, for me, the act of hugging was complicated. As a child who followed me as an adult, it didn't represent love or compassion. It did not express comfort to me. I don't want to live in that past, clinging to the idea that being emotionally distant is acceptable. I want God to continue changing me, helping me grow beyond the limitations of my upbringing. I'd like the same for you.

Compassion requires vulnerability, and I've learned that vulnerability is a strength, not a weakness. Being able to hug, love deeply, and express emotion is part of reflecting the heart of Jesus. It's uncomfortable for me, but I push through because God is teaching me that true marksmen strive to aim higher and love deeper.

The Bible tells us exactly how to approach this in Ephesians 4:32: "Instead, be kind to each other, tenderhearted, forgiving one another, just as God through Christ has forgiven you." It's clear that being tenderhearted and forgiving is at the core of our walk with God, and it's something we must embody daily.

By choosing to push past my own discomfort, I am breaking a cycle. I am setting a new standard of compassion for my family. My hope is that they will grow up knowing what love looks like—not the tough exterior I once thought was strength. I'm learning that real strength comes from opening up, showing affection, and allowing the love of Christ to flow through me to others.

BREAKING THROUGH PERSONAL BARRIERS

Compassion, at its core, requires forgiveness. I've had to forgive so much—years of hurt, abuse, betrayal, and the insecurities that bring self-loathing because of my past. Not only did I need to forgive those who wronged me, but I also had to forgive myself for the harm I caused others. This kind of forgiveness is not something we can accomplish on our own; it has to be supernatural. If God is not holding your mistakes against you, why are you?

Unforgiveness is like a prison that keeps many men from walking in true freedom. It holds us back from being the marksmen God has called us to be—the men who walk in compassion, love, and truth. Without forgiveness, we are weighed down and unable to move forward in our relationships and spiritual growth. We are stuck, unable to reflect the character of Christ to others. Matthew 6:14-15 also reinforces this: "If you forgive those who sin against you, your heavenly Father will forgive you. But if you refuse to forgive others, your Father will not forgive your sins."

I encourage you to look deep within yourself. Ask God to reveal the places where you need to forgive—whether it's others or even yourself—and allow Him to change your heart. Peter's words resonate deeply here: "Don't just pretend to love others. Really love them" (Romans 12:9). We cannot genuinely love and show compassion if unforgiveness is holding us back. It takes the transformative power of God to truly love others as Christ does.

As men, we often focus on our gifts and achievements, but what truly matters is the fruit we produce. We don't need more gifted men leading—we need more *fruitful men*, displaying the fruits of the Spirit as described in Galatians 5:22-23: "But the Holy Spirit produces this kind of fruit in our lives: love, joy, peace, patience, kindness, goodness, faithfulness, gentleness, and self-control." Becoming a fruitful man with a heart of compassion, like Jesus, will make a lasting difference in how we disciple others and how we impact the world around us.

In closing, compassion flows from a heart that is free from bitterness and unforgiveness. Let God work on your heart, and as you are filled with His love and grace, allow that to flow through you into your relationships, family, workplace, and community. Compassion isn't just about what we feel; it's about how we act and how we live. Through Christ's example, we can show the world what true compassion looks like—compassion that forgives, loves, and transforms.

PRACTICAL APPLICATION
LIVING OUT COMPASSION

Biblical compassion calls us to action, to live with a heart rooted in Christ's love and forgiveness. Here are some practical steps to help you grow in compassion:

1) **Pray for a Heart of Compassion:** Ask God to soften your heart and fill it with His love for others. Ask the Holy Spirit to help you see people through His eyes, beyond their flaws, to their needs.

2) **Practice Forgiveness:** Identify areas where unforgiveness is holding you back. Let go of bitterness and choose to forgive those who have wronged you. Remember, forgiveness is essential for compassion.

3) **Serve With Sacrifice:** Compassion requires action. Look for opportunities to serve others, even when it's

inconvenient. Whether it's helping a friend in need or showing kindness to a stranger, be willing to step out of your comfort zone.

4) **Listen With Empathy:** Sometimes, people don't need solutions—they need someone to listen. Practice being present for others and bearing their burdens. As Galatians 6:2 says, *"Share each other's burdens, and in this way obey the law of Christ."*

5) **Model Jesus's Compassion in Your Relationships:** In your marriage, friendships, workplace, and community, show the love of Christ by being kind, patient, and forgiving. Let others see that you live with compassion, just as Jesus did.

CHAPTER 14
MEN OF FAITH

The Bible asks, "Many claim to have unfailing love, but a faithful person who can find? (Proverbs 20:6, NIV). This verse highlights the difficulty of proving yourself to be a praying faithful man. Faithfulness is a challenging character trait, requiring consistency and commitment in all seasons of life. As men, we each have our strengths and weaknesses, good days and bad ones. We struggle to find consistency in our daily lives and sometimes go through the days as if we are going through the motions. I have an autopilot setting. At times, it is like the car is driving itself to the next task, next meeting, and next responsibility. I don't even remember how I got to where I was going. It just happens. Men must be faithful, as faithfulness is one of the most vital characteristics defining a man of God. No matter how routine, when we approach our daily activities with the character trait of faithfulness, we will be more successful in becoming more like Jesus.

A man's faithfulness speaks to his loyalty, steadfastness, and reliability. He is a man people can depend on, and this is the kind of man others want to follow.

In today's culture, faithfulness is often diminished and undervalued. Marriage is sometimes treated as a temporary arrangement or a transactional relationship they check in and out of.

Many men shy away consistently from hard work, discipline, and dependability. These are key character traits we don't want to overlook. Loyalty and commitment, especially to churches or families, often take a back seat to work and recreation. Some men are more faithful to their favorite sports teams than their churches and daily commitments. I have found it much easier to be faithful to my career than to other responsibilities and obligations. That unwillingness to faithfully challenge my commitments was rooted in insecurities I tried to hide. I had no issues being faithful to what I am good at, what comes naturally to me, or recreational things that bring me joy, but it's the areas that challenge us the most that are often the ones we most need to commit to.

The Bible compels us to live at a higher standard. Proverbs 3:3 (NIV) reminds us: "Let love and faithfulness never leave you; bind them around your neck, write them on the tablet of your heart."

I love how this verse combines love with faithfulness, as they go hand in hand. When we love what we do or when what we do provides for those we love, we are more likely to remain faithful. We read in the previous chapters that learning how to love is a sign of growth and maturity.

Our character is meant to be a part of who we are, not something we project for the world to see when trying to be someone. So many men I know are so used to being a public personality that they lose themselves privately. When no one is around, our thoughts can hurt us and make us want to quit.

Being faithful in our relationships, work, ministry, and walk with God is essential for a disciplined life of faith. As marksmen consistently aim for their targets, we must be resilient and push ourselves to endure. The Bible is full of examples of men struggling to remain faithful, reminding us that faithfulness is not always easy. Ultimately, there is only One who is truly faithful—Jesus. He modeled perfect faithfulness by His unwavering commitment to His Father's will.

In the Garden of Gethsemane, we see Jesus's humanity. He was fully God, yet he took on man's weaknesses minus our sinful nature.

Though He was under immense pressure, sweating drops of blood, He stayed faithful to God's plan when he said, "Not my will, but yours be done" (Luke 22:42, NIV). Jesus didn't give in to His emotions or seek an easier way. His faithfulness led Him to endure the cross. As men of God, we are called to follow His example and remain faithful even in difficult seasons. Steadfast faithfulness is tested in times of hardship, like gold being refined by fire.

PERSONAL REFLECTIONS: STAYING FAITHFUL THROUGH CHALLENGES

Looking back at my life, I see many moments when I was tempted to take the easy way out. It's easy to seek an exit when things get tough. As long as we believe there are options to avoid hardship, we'll always wonder if we should quit. Options can become the enemy of success. It made all the difference when I removed those options and remained faithful. Specific commitments in life—our faith, families, and responsibilities—are non-negotiable. We must stay faithful and see them through.

That struggling mindset of needing to seek other options reminds me of when I took my son to Disneyland when he was four. We had a great time, but he was afraid of some of the rides. I convinced him to try the Tower of Terror, thinking he'd enjoy it if he gave it a chance. As a kid, I was afraid of rides, and I wanted him to be different—to be fearless. But in my immaturity, I projected my own insecurities onto him. As we stood in line, I could see the fear on his face. Instead of being honest, I told him it was just an elevator ride that goes up and down, leaving out the parts about the sudden drops and thrills.

This was a mistake. After the ride, which was traumatizing for him, it took him years to get on another thrill ride. I had tried to trick him into becoming something he wasn't ready for—just as my own father had done to me. I realized I was projecting my insecurities onto him, hoping he'd be a better version of who I was as a kid. That's when I understood that forcing him through fear was not the way to build courage or faithfulness.

Looking back, I realize I should have let him face the challenge in his own time. What if God tricked us into following Him? Thankfully, He doesn't. Jesus tells us straight: "In this world you will have trouble. But take heart! I have overcome the world" (John 16:33, NIV). God is honest with us—following Him is difficult, but He promises to be with us every step of the way. When we're young in faith, we may be tempted to back out when fear arises. But as men, we must understand that life—much like that ride—will have ups and downs, but we must remain faithful and endure to the end.

This story with my son at Disneyland may seem like a silly example. It is embarrassing for me to talk about since it's terrible parenting. Still, it taught me how important it is to face challenges head-on. It's okay to let a child decide when they're ready for something, but as men, we need to stop looking for exits. I later used it as a lesson for my son when he was a teenager. It wasn't about the ride—it was about teaching him not to let fear stop him from trying something new. You won't know who you really are when you live in fear. For us as men, faithfulness means not letting fear or challenges cause us to step away from what God has called us to do.

MY JOURNEY IN MINISTRY: LEARNING TO STAY

I've been with the same church since I was seventeen years old and have realized that this isn't common in today's world. Meeting pastors who have stayed in one place for that long is rare. I have faithfully served in every area of this church right up until the day I became the lead pastor. Looking back, I see that God was shaping me through every experience, giving me perspective as I walked through the ups and downs and all the hurt, disappointments, and challenges. Over the years, we experienced several church splits; people we cared about cut us off because they were upset with the pastor. They were mad we did not leave. It was like the movie Jerry Maguire[9], where he quits and expects a whole bunch of people to go with him. In the twenty-plus years of being at the church, I even had my share of disagreements with leadership. There were moments when I felt mistreated and disrespected, to the point that other pastors and leaders advised me to leave—especially during one of the most challenging seasons when it was hurting me to stay. The years of work my wife and I put into the church seemed undone, and there was nothing I could do about it.

---

9 Cameron Crow, *Jerry Maguire* (December 13, 1996; Culver City, CA: TriStar Pictures).

It's hard to stay faithful when things happen outside of your control. But despite everything, I wouldn't change a thing. The lessons I learned from the good, the bad, and the ugly were worth the price. Today, I have the privilege of continuing the work my pastor started—not as an outsider coming in but as someone who shared in the church's legacy.

What kept me grounded was seeking God in prayer during those times when I was tempted to quit. Every time I was at a breaking point, God would tell me to endure. He was building character in me—the kind of character that can push through adversity. I often wonder what might have happened if I had followed my feelings instead of God's direction. I tell people it takes faith to go, but it also takes faith to stay and push through.

What really matters under challenging seasons is discerning what God is saying. I know this is a risky thing to say because, over the years, I've heard many people use the phrase "God told me . . . ." When every detail of their lives is constantly sourced from what God told them, it implies that God frequently changes His mind, which is not likely. In fact, it's improbable—if not impossible. I have found people are more likely to mistake their own thoughts, wants, or preferences as His and don't take the time to seek clear direction or work through adversity. They simply say, "God told me"—so much so that they end up doing the exact opposite of what He "told" them to do last week.

I've found that waiting on the Lord, praying, fasting, and confirming His direction in the Word, is the way to go. It's not always easy. God tried to make it easy for Adam, but it messed everything up. Adam was given one command and could not do it. The easy road is not always the right road, and simpler roads are only sometimes better. I believe He challenges us because He knows we need to learn how to remain faithful.

The church I pastor belongs to God, and He wanted to build specific character traits in me to lead. Looking back, I now realize that many of the trials I faced were part of His plan. I didn't understand it at the time, but now it's clear why the Lord didn't release me or want me to leave during those difficult moments because I needed them to become the man I am today. I always tell people I thank God for the gutter because, without it, I would have never called on Jesus.

I share this to encourage you to be faithful to what God has entrusted to you. Take your time, and do not run or bounce around when challenges arise. Instead, get rooted in the right environment and let wisdom take its course. Without time and faithfulness, we will never grow. As one of my mentors once told me, "You can pass the test now, or you can run, but you'll only find yourself right back at the test again."

The Lord is faithful, and He finishes the work He starts. As the Bible says, "He who began a good work in you will carry it on to completion" (Philippians 1:6, NIV). Remember this when you have to decide what to do next.

PRACTICAL APPLICATION
FAITHFULNESS IN EVERYDAY LIFE

Being faithful brings value to every area of a man's life. It's showing up every day, doing your job to the best of your ability, coming home to your family, and interacting with your community in a way that brings glory to God. Faithfulness is about consistency—honoring your commitments and being true to your word.

In marriage, it means staying loyal to your vows, even when times get tough. At work, it means giving your best effort, even when no one is watching. In our walk with God, it means consistently spending time in His Word and in prayer, even when it feels like nothing is happening.

Faithfulness requires perseverance. It's doing the right thing, trusting that God sees what others do not. Lamentations 3:22-23 reminds us, "The faithful love of the LORD never ends! His mercies never cease. Great is his faithfulness; his mercies begin afresh each morning." Just as God is faithful to us, we are called to live out that same faithfulness in every part of our lives.

Faithfulness to the Mission

As men, we are called to be faithful to the mission God has given us. The apostle Paul said, "Now it is required that those who have been given a trust must prove faithful" (1 Corinthians 4:2, NIV). Every role we hold—as husbands, fathers, workers, and servants of Christ—requires us to remain faithful. Our calling is to endure, stay focused on what matters, and glorify God in all we do.

Faithfulness in Action

Living a life of faithfulness requires more than just good intentions; it requires consistent action in every area of our lives. Here are some practical ways to cultivate and demonstrate faithfulness:

1) **Be Faithful in the Small Things:** It's easy to be faithful in big moments when everyone is watching, but steadfast faithfulness is revealed in how we handle small, everyday tasks. Luke 16:10 reminds us, "If you are faithful in little things,

you will be faithful in large ones." Start by showing up consistently, whether at work, with your family, or in ministry.

2) **Honor Your Commitments:** Faithfulness means sticking to your word, even when it's hard or inconvenient. Whether it's a promise to your family, a commitment at church, or a responsibility at work, follow through. Ecclesiastes 5:5 says, "It is better to say nothing than to make a promise and not keep it."

3) **Remain Steadfast in Trials:** Faithfulness is often tested in seasons of hardship. When you face challenges, don't be quick to look for an escape route. James 1:12 says, "God blesses those who patiently endure testing and temptation." Trust that God is working even when things are complicated, and be faithful through the trial.

4) **Commit to Personal Growth:** Stay faithful in your relationship with God through regular prayer, Bible study, and devotion. Colossians 3:16 encourages us to "Let the message about Christ, in all its richness, fill your lives." Personal devotion keeps you grounded in your faith and strengthens you to remain faithful in all areas of life.

5) **Persevere in Relationships:** Whether in marriage, friendships, or family, relationships take work. Be committed to nurturing those relationships through thick and thin. Proverbs 17:17 says, "A friend is always loyal, and a brother is born to help in time of need." Show your faithfulness by being present and supportive, even when times are tough.

6) **Remain Faithful to the Mission:** God has given each of us a mission—whether in ministry, family, or work—and we

are called to be faithful to that mission. First Corinthians 4:2 (NIV) states, "Now it is required that those who have been given a trust must prove faithful." No matter what role you hold, fulfill it with faithfulness and integrity.

ASK YOURSELF:

- How can I demonstrate faithfulness in the small things today?
- Where have I been tempted to give up, and how can I remain steadfast?
- What commitments have I made that need renewed attention and effort?

CHAPTER 15
IT ALL COMES TOGETHER

After reading this book, I pray you feel inspired—or, better yet, challenged. At the heart of everything I have written is a call for us men to become better followers of Jesus. That has to be our central goal. As men, we endure a lot and carry so much, and we need to be close to Jesus. All of us are called to lead, which is how God created us. The best way to achieve your goals in this life is to keep your focus on Jesus.

The journey of putting a book together was a challenge for me. I can't tell you how many times I started to write a book that just wouldn't come together. I thought I would never be able to write. Yet, this book flowed in a way I can't fully explain. There's just a time and season for everything. I know this one is meant for you. For some of you, this is the first time you've been challenged in this way. For others, it's a reminder of who you are and what God has already spoken to you.

The amazing thing about following Jesus is that there is no perfect cookie-cutter system. Every journey is unique, and the words in this book will motivate and inspire you in your own personal way. This book is just a guide to help point you in the right direction, but only God can cause your life to change. That's the truth every man needs to hear: only God Himself can transform your life—from your emotions to your relationships to your work and your view of yourself. No pastor, mentor, accountability partner, spouse, friend, or other person can unlock your full potential without you connecting directly with God. Only God holds the keys to your personal growth.

As Paul writes in 1 Corinthians 3:6-7 (NIV), "I planted the seed, Apollos watered it, but God has been making it grow. So neither the one who plants nor the one who waters is anything, but only God, who makes things grow."

God's ability to lead you to grow is why we men must be challenged to follow Jesus's example every day, in every way, no matter how difficult it feels. He is the key to everything, and we must find a way.

So, what now? All the lessons from this book point to a simple answer: do something with the knowledge and wisdom you've gained. To be a disciple and follower of Jesus is not to sit back in idle comfort but to shift gears and live it out. A true disciple of Christ applies what he has learned and, equally important, passes it on to disciple others.

Jesus told His disciples, "Give as freely as you have received!" (Matthew 10:8) This passage reminds us to take the lessons and teachings we receive and pass them on.

One of your first steps is to find other men and talk through the lessons you've learned. Encourage one another to accept the challenge of becoming better followers of Jesus. Hold each other accountable and motivate each other as the scripture says, "Let us think of ways to motivate one another to acts of love and good works" (Hebrews 10:24). We are to push each other, encourage each other, and help each other.

This is the way of the marksmen: the continuation of the work of Jesus. He took a small group of dedicated followers and changed the world. That is what happens when men act upon the calling God gives us. We see entire households and communities transformed. When God saved me, He didn't just bless me—He blessed all those who would come after me. The cycle is broken, and my children and their children are blessed through my willingness to be transformed by His message. The generations of my family will have an opportunity to expand on the work He started for me. Because of what He has done, my decisions can set up a new legacy for my family. My name now carries a new meaning and purpose. My family's legacy included a history of addiction, anger, and failure, but through His grace, I've been brought into His family. Now, my legacy is tied to the history I see in Scripture.

This is what the Word tells us: "Once you had no identity as a people; now you are God's people. Once you received no mercy; now you have received God's mercy" (1 Peter 2:10). When you follow Christ, you become co-heirs to the promise—no longer a slave to sin but set free. "This means that anyone who belongs to Christ has become a new person. The old life is gone; a new life has begun!" (2 Corinthians 5:17). These verses tell us what is possible when we trust Jesus and follow His way.

I am a collector, so I have a lot of collectibles. My office, house, and garage are full of things that remind me of who I am. When you walk into any room where I have creative control, you'll see comics, sports memorabilia, and ticket stubs from games

I've been to. I set these little things around me as reminders to be myself and live in freedom. People have come into my office criticizing me for having so much comic book stuff, but those stories inspire me. I could preach a sermon about every character: Iron Man and his addiction, the Hulk with his anger, Spider-Man struggling with poverty and feeling out of place, Batman dealing with trauma—should I go on? These stories have meaning to me.

Setting up visual reminders is why, at our church, we give out a compass to men who go through the discipleship process to remind them of these principles: put God first, deny self, value family, and uphold ministry. When we had our Christian clothing company, we wanted people to express their faith by what they wore. We even started a Christian music label because music helps us in our identity. Do anything you can to keep yourself grounded in your need for Jesus. Find reminders that help you live the way you're called to live.

When I was a teenager, that reminder was the "What Would Jesus Do?" wristband. There was even a season early in my career when I wrote "Higher Purpose" on my hand with a pen to remind me that all the hard work was serving a purpose greater than I realized. I'm visual like that. I encourage you, men, to do whatever is necessary to stay locked in on this mission to follow Jesus.

Ultimately, what matters is that more men rise in our churches and take their place as the leaders they are called to be. Become the father, brother, husband, and son God designed you to be. He has set you apart for such a time as this.

I want to leave you with preacher one-liners to help you on your journey. We preachers love these little sayings that offer words of wisdom to help you along the way.

First, work hard and rest well. Resting well is an area I struggle with. While I have no problem putting in hard work—I take pride in being diligent—I believe there's no substitute for hard work. I don't buy the "work smarter—not harder" philosophy; I believe in both. However, we must also learn to rest well. The Bible teaches us the importance of rest. In Matthew 11:28-30 (NIV), Jesus says, "Come to me, all you who are weary and burdened, and I will give you rest. Take my yoke upon you and learn from me, for I am gentle and humble in heart, and you will find rest for your souls. For my yoke is easy, and my burden is light." Learning to unplug and recharge extends your life and leads to a healthier lifestyle, which allows you to accomplish more and be happy.

Second, trust God and trust the process. That's a direct quote from my nephew, Deandre Carter, who has been one of the great inspirations in my life. He plays in the NFL, and his journey was filled with adversity and challenges, yet he persevered through each. His story is amazing. I admire his dedication to living out his dreams and what it took to carve out a ten-year NFL career. He had many reasons to quit or change his goals but did not. Many people want to skip the process and jump straight to the destination, but there are no shortcuts. Trust God in whatever you must go through to become the man you aspire to be. Proverbs 3:5-6 (NIV) reminds us, "Trust in the Lord with all your heart and lean not on your own understanding; in all your ways submit to him, and he will make your paths straight."

Finally, follow the Way—follow Jesus. I want it to sink in. There's no better guidance than that. Take it to heart. In John 14:6 (NIV), Jesus declares, "I am the way and the truth and the life. No one comes to the Father except through me."

There is no other way, no higher calling, no greater purpose, and no treasure more valuable than following Jesus.